MERCY

A BIBLE STUDY GUIDE FOR CATHOLICS

MERCY

A BIBLE STUDY GUIDE FOR CATHOLICS

FR. MITCH PACWA, S.J.

Our Sunday Visitor Publishing Division
Our Sunday Visitor, Inc.
Huntington, IN 46750

Nihil Obstat
Msgr. Michael Heintz, Ph.D.
Censor Librorum

Imprimatur
✠ Kevin C. Rhoades
Bishop of Fort Wayne-South Bend
January 23, 2015

The *Nihil Obstat* and *Imprimatur* are official declarations that a book is free from doctrinal or moral error. It is not implied that those who have granted the *Nihil Obstat* and *Imprimatur* agree with the contents, opinions, or statements expressed.

Every reasonable effort has been made to determine copyright holders of excerpted materials and to secure permissions as needed. If any copyrighted materials have been inadvertently used in this work without proper credit being given in one form or another, please notify Our Sunday Visitor in writing so that future printings of this work may be corrected accordingly.

ISBN: 978-1-61278-791-6 (Inventory No. T1597)
eISBN: 978-1-61278-361-1
LCCN: 2015931938

Cover design: Lindsey Riesen
Cover art: The Crosiers
Interior design: Sherri L. Hoffman
Interior art: iStockPhoto.com

PRINTED IN THE UNITED STATES OF AMERICA

To Fr. Robert Thesing, S.J.,
whose calm intellect inspired me
to study well, and to engage others
with knowledge rather than my temper.
God bless his long pastoral service
of many years of care
and mercy for others.

CONTENTS

HOW TO USE THIS STUDY GUIDE IN A GROUP

This is an interactive study guide. It can be read with profit either alone or as part of a group Bible study. Below are suggestions for the use of this book in a group.

WHAT YOU WILL NEED FOR EVERY SESSION

- This study guide
- A Bible
- A notebook

- **Before Session 1, members of the group are encouraged to read the Introduction and Session 1 and to complete all the exercises in both.** They should bring this study guide with them to the group session.
- **Begin the session with prayer** (for example, see the Chaplet of Divine Mercy on page 119).
- **Invite one person in the group to read one of the Scripture passages included in this session's material.**
- **Allow five minutes of silent reflection on the passage.** This allows the group's members to quiet their inner thoughts and to center themselves on the lesson to be discussed.
- **Catechesis:** Give all members a chance to share some point that they have learned about mercy. Was this something new or a new insight into something? Was there anything that raised a question? (Allow fifteen to twenty minutes for this.)
- **Discussion:** Use the discussion questions at the end of the session chapter to begin a deeper grasp of the material covered in the session. (Allow fifteen to twenty minutes for this.)

- **Conclusion:** Have all members of the group summarize the key concepts they learned and discussed about mercy in the session. Assign the next session as homework, to be completed before the next group session.

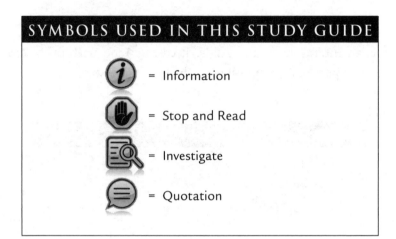

SYMBOLS USED IN THIS STUDY GUIDE

= Information

= Stop and Read

= Investigate

= Quotation

ACKNOWLEDGMENTS

Unless otherwise noted, the Scripture citations used in this work are taken from the *Catholic Edition of the Revised Standard Version of the Bible* (RSV), copyright © 1965, 1966 by the Division of Christian Education of the National Council of the Churches of Christ in the United States of America. Used by permission. All rights reserved. Where noted, other Scripture citations are from the *Revised Standard Version of the Bible — Second Catholic Edition* (Ignatius Edition), designated as RSV-SCE. Copyright © 2006 National Council of the Churches of Christ in the United States of America. Used by permission. All rights reserved.

Quotations from papal statements, Vatican II, and other Vatican documents are copyrighted, © 2014, by Libreria Editrice Vaticana.

The English translations of the Lord's Prayer (Our Father) and the Apostles' Creed are by the International Consultation on English Texts or the English Language Liturgical Consultation.

The instructions on how to pray the Chaplet of Divine Mercy are courtesy of the Marian Fathers of the Immaculate Conception of the Blessed Virgin Mary (http://thedivinemercy.org/message/devotions /praythechaplet.php).

INTRODUCTION

"In Christ and through Christ, God also becomes especially visible in His mercy; that is to say, there is emphasized that attribute of the divinity which the Old Testament, using various concepts and terms, already defined as 'mercy.' Christ confers on the whole of the Old Testament tradition about God's mercy a definitive meaning. Not only does He speak of it and explain it by the use of comparisons and parables, but above all He Himself makes it incarnate and personifies it. He Himself, in a certain sense, is mercy. To the person who sees it in Him — and finds it in Him — God becomes 'visible' in a particular way as the Father who is rich in mercy."

— POPE ST. JOHN PAUL II, *Dives in Misericordia* (n. 2)

This Bible study centers on the history of the development of Israel's experience of mercy, with a final look at how God's mercy is embodied in Christ. Mercy does not appear very often in the early history of Israel. Israel's experiences of breaking God's commandments and then receiving his mercy is key to the slow process of understanding mercy. For the most part, mercy is shown within the context of the people of Israel accepting the covenant with God. The covenant was a mutual commitment of the Lord God to Israel and of Israel to be his people. Despite their commitment, Israel sinned many times by breaking the commandments that formed key stipulations that gave guidance to their relationship with God and one another. However, precisely because the Lord bound himself to Israel with covenant love, his commitment opened the way for them to find mercy when they were unfaithful to covenantal committed love. Mercy became the way they learned that God's love is more powerful than their sin.

This study cannot cover all of the occurrences and developments of mercy throughout the Bible. However, coming to a deeper understanding of Israel's struggle to learn about mercy within their covenant relationship with God may give contemporary people some insight into serving the Lord and our brothers and sisters around the world by helping them rediscover mercy in our merciless time in history.

CONSIDER

Pope St. John Paul II wrote a cycle of three encyclicals, one on each Person of the Trinity. He entitled the encyclical on God the Father *Dives in Misericordia*, or *Rich in Mercy*. It is difficult not to see this encyclical in light of his background in Poland during World War II. He did forced labor at a quarry just across the railroad tracks from the convent and grave where St. Faustina Kowalska died and was buried, just eleven months before the Nazi invasion of Poland. He frequently stopped to pray in the convent chapel, the only church permitted by the Nazis to remain open in Kraków. Already, the sisters were leading the Chaplet of Divine Mercy that St. Faustina had received during her visions. The prayer "Have mercy on us and on the whole world" deeply helped the future saint realize that he needed to seek God's mercy not only for himself but also for the Nazi oppressors who were deporting Jewish neighbors, killing his friends among the Polish underground, undermining the culture, and appropriating the nation's resources.

Including the Nazis in this prayer drew him to the principle of solidarity. He understand that rather than dividing humans into enemies and friends, we are in solidarity with every human being, even our opponents, because we all need mercy and we all possess a human dignity that is bestowed by God directly on each person.

Not only did St. John Paul make this principle a salient element of his theology, but he also gave his episcopal approbation to Sister Faustina's diary, later beatifying her and then canonizing her. In so doing, he paved the way for the popularization of the Chaplet of Divine Mercy and the recognition of Divine Mercy Sunday, on whose eve he passed into God's glory.

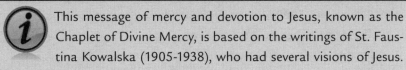

CHAPLET OF DIVINE MERCY

(i) This message of mercy and devotion to Jesus, known as the Chaplet of Divine Mercy, is based on the writings of St. Faustina Kowalska (1905-1938), who had several visions of Jesus. In the visions, Jesus presented three main themes: to ask for the mercy of God, to trust in Christ's mercy, and to show mercy to others and act as a conduit for God's mercy toward them. (See page 119 for directions on praying the chaplet.)

STUDY

The people of Poland embraced the devotion to the Divine Mercy, and it became common to see pictures of Jesus the Divine Mercy displayed next to images of the Sacred Heart of Jesus in churches throughout the country. This phenomenon shows the continuity rather than any disjuncture between these two very influential devotions.

SACRED HEART OF JESUS

(i) While homage to the Sacred Heart dates back to at least the thirteenth century, the devotion as we know it today owes its origin to St. Margaret Mary Alacoque (1647–1690), a nun of the Order of the Visitation of Holy Mary, who saw visions of Jesus in which he outlined the devotion, which includes reception of Holy Communion on the first Friday of each month, Eucharistic Adoration during a "holy hour" on Thursdays, and the celebration of the feast of the Sacred Heart.

St. Margaret Mary reported that those who follow the devotion would have the benefits of the following promises:

1. I will give them all the graces necessary for their state of life.
2. I will give peace in their families.
3. I will console them in all their troubles.
4. I will be their refuge in life and especially in death.

Continued on next page . . .

. . . *continued from previous page*

5. I will abundantly bless all their undertakings.
6. Sinners shall find in my Heart the source and infinite ocean of mercy.
7. Tepid souls shall become fervent.
8. Fervent souls shall rise speedily to great perfection.
9. I will bless those places wherein the image of my Sacred Heart shall be exposed and venerated.
10. I will give to priests the power to touch the most hardened hearts.
11. Persons who propagate this devotion shall have their names eternally written in my Heart.
12. In the excess of the mercy of my Heart, I promise you that my all powerful love will grant to all those who will receive Communion on the First Fridays, for nine consecutive months, the grace of final repentance: they will not die in my displeasure, nor without receiving the sacraments; and my Heart will be their secure refuge in that last hour.

If Divine Mercy and the Sacred Heart are so close in spirit, why did the Lord reveal the Divine Mercy, and why did it take hold of the laity with such ease?

The answer may lie in the contexts for the two devotions. The Sacred Heart was revealed when Jansenism arose and inspired a harsh, cold understanding of Catholic life. In contrast to Jansenism, the Sacred Heart of Jesus revealed himself as a burning furnace of love, who called everyone to an intense love of him in return and to a love of neighbor.

JANSENISM

Jansenism is a heretical teaching that focuses on the essential depravity of humanity and emphasizes original sin and predestination. Its belief in predestination, the concept that only a few select will be saved, denies the role of free will in the acceptance and use of grace. It derives its name from Dutch theologian Cornelius Jansen, who died in 1638.

The Divine Mercy was revealed between the two World Wars and during the rise of totalitarian regimes across Europe, and later in the Middle East and East Asia. Though modern people since the early eighteenth century have stated that religion has been the greatest cause of war in human history, the facts show that secular, atheistic, and anti-religious governments have made religious wars, as bad as they are, seem tiny conflicts in comparison. Wars and persecutions originating with Christianity (including the Crusades, the Inquisition, and the witch trials), waged primarily between the mid-eleventh and mid-seventeenth centuries, account for 2.65 million deaths, using the more generous figure of 1 million deaths in the Crusades. In contrast, secular wars began with the anti-religious French Revolution and the consequent Napoleonic Wars, in which 2.5 million people died, while World War I caused 20 million deaths and World War II 50 million deaths.

Atheistic governments went far beyond these figures: the Soviet Union killed 61.9 million of its own citizens; Communist China 76.7 million citizens; and their satellites another 20 million. Altogether, the secular and atheistic regimes account for the deaths of 308 million people in the twentieth century. Furthermore, the number of abortions is over 200 million and climbing worldwide. Not only is religion not even a close contender for being responsible for the greatest amount of violence in history, but the regimes that reject religion set themselves up for a level of cruelty, violence, and death precisely because they reject the limitations that religion sets on their moral behavior (see http://www.hawaii.edu/powerkills/welcome.html).

In light of this violent and vicious aspect of twentieth-century history, the reason for the revelation of the Divine Mercy becomes absolutely clear: the twentieth century was the most merciless in history. The merciless quality of modern life is the quality that Jesus the Divine Mercy addresses by calling modern people to receive his mercy and share it with every other person: "Have mercy on us and on the whole world."

A rediscovery of God's role in history, the importance and benefit of authentic religion, and the need for merciful forgiveness of our rejection of God and his laws will be a tremendous boon for modern people to learn, to extend mercy to fellow human beings equally made in the image and likeness of God. Whether their faces show the coldly efficient hatred of Nazis and communists or the intense hatred of terrorists, we pray, "Have mercy on us and on the whole world."

Such is the earnestness with which we begin this study of mercy in the history of the ancient people of God — Israel — and for the New Israel: the Church.

Session 1

HUMAN MERCY

"Jesus is all mercy, Jesus is all love: he is God made man. Each of us, each one of us, is that little lost lamb, the coin that was mislaid; each one of us is that son who has squandered his freedom on false idols, illusions of happiness, and has lost everything. But God does not forget us, the Father never abandons us. He is a patient father, always waiting for us! He respects our freedom, but he remains faithful forever. And when we come back to him, he welcomes us like children into his house, for he never ceases, not for one instant, to wait for us with love. And his heart rejoices over every child who returns. He is celebrating because he is joy. God has this joy, when one of us sinners goes to him and asks his forgiveness."

— POPE FRANCIS, Angelus address (September 15, 2013)

The main focus of study in this book will be God's mercy, but we will begin with a study of the passages that treat human mercy for two reasons. First, much of the language of mercy in the Bible is taken from human experience. The finite nature of human beings cannot comprehend the infinite nature of God: he remains eternally beyond the scope of limited human minds. Therefore, people use a variety of images and words from everyday life that become analogies for God's relationship with humanity and the world. It's somewhat analogous to the relationship between a dog and its master. A few words, such as the dog's name, "eat," "come," and "sit" in a well-trained dog, will elicit appropriate actions and barks, whines, and facial expressions. However, only in a cartoon, never in real life, will the dog speak a sentence of actual words. The gap between a dog and a person is not nearly as wide as the gap between a human and God's infinity, but we "bark" in words, sentences, and thoughts to the best of our ability.

In this book, we will transliterate the terms for mercy from the original languages and at various times explain their meaning.

The second reason we begin with a study of human mercy is that the limitations of human mercy point to the need of God's mercy as a superior form and source. God's mercy is in complete union with his justice, which is a perennial conundrum for limited humans to manage. In fact, we will see that frequently people seek mercy from fellow human beings by asking God to bestow a gift of mercy upon the one who is able to show mercy. The history of God's mercy with Israel in the Old Testament will be the theme of later chapters, but for now we will examine people who either show or fail to show human mercy.

CONSIDER

The first group is composed of those who do not show mercy because they are wicked. Two proverbs point to an interesting and generally true principle: The wicked are not capable of mercy.

The first of these proverbs begins with an observation of the way people relate to the domestic animals under their control: "A righteous man has regard for the life of his beast, but the mercy [Hebrew *rahamei*; Septuagint *splangcha*] of the wicked is cruel" (Prov 12:10).

A person who is righteous "has regard" for his domestic animals. The Hebrew literally says, "He knows the soul [*nephesh*] of his beast." Any decent farmer or rancher who works closely with animals pays close attention to changes in diet, facial expression, and demeanor and stays alert to these signals that indicate illness, exhaustion, or injury. Decent people who work with animals recognize the partnership and are aware of the animal's dependence on the humans. The Septuagint version of Scripture translates "knows the soul" as *oiktirei*, meaning "have compassion," as a good interpretation of the phrase.

20

The wicked might speak of their "mercy," but any decent person looking at their behavior will recognize that it is in reality a "cruel" (Hebrew *akzari*) action. Interestingly, the Septuagint word for "cruel" is *aneleemona* (literally, "merciless"). The Hebrew term for "mercy" here is *rahamim*, a term derived from the Hebrew word for "womb." The womb is an all-encompassing reality for a baby, and that is one of the most common terms for mercy in the Old Testament.

The second proverb reads: "The soul of the wicked desires evil; his neighbor finds no mercy [Hebrew *lò yehan*; Septuagint *ouk eleethesetai*] in his eyes" (Prov 21:10).

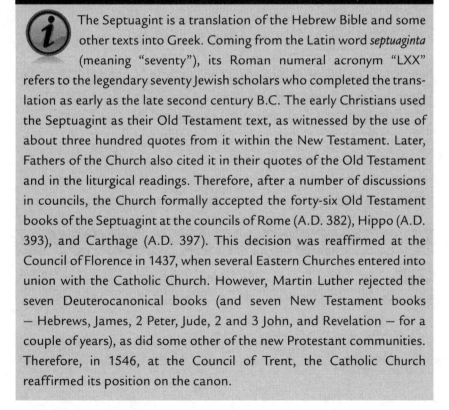

SEPTUAGINT (OR "LXX")

The Septuagint is a translation of the Hebrew Bible and some other texts into Greek. Coming from the Latin word *septuaginta* (meaning "seventy"), its Roman numeral acronym "LXX" refers to the legendary seventy Jewish scholars who completed the translation as early as the late second century B.C. The early Christians used the Septuagint as their Old Testament text, as witnessed by the use of about three hundred quotes from it within the New Testament. Later, Fathers of the Church also cited it in their quotes of the Old Testament and in the liturgical readings. Therefore, after a number of discussions in councils, the Church formally accepted the forty-six Old Testament books of the Septuagint at the councils of Rome (A.D. 382), Hippo (A.D. 393), and Carthage (A.D. 397). This decision was reaffirmed at the Council of Florence in 1437, when several Eastern Churches entered into union with the Catholic Church. However, Martin Luther rejected the seven Deuterocanonical books (and seven New Testament books — Hebrews, James, 2 Peter, Jude, 2 and 3 John, and Revelation — for a couple of years), as did some other of the new Protestant communities. Therefore, in 1546, at the Council of Trent, the Catholic Church reaffirmed its position on the canon.

The desire for evil deeds on the part of a wicked person blinds him to ever showing mercy to a neighbor. The word for "finds no mercy" in Hebrew is "he will not be shown grace." The Hebrew root, *hanan*, means to "be gracious," or "show grace or favor."

The proverbs just cited, like most of the verses in Proverbs 10-29, each stands alone. However, some parts of the Wisdom books are "instructions" — that is, short essays that teach and try to motivate the reader to action. Sirach 28:1-5 is part of such an instruction meant to motivate people to obey God's commandments and forgive other people.

 Stop here and read **Sirach 28:1-2** in your own Bible.

These verses begin with a statement of fact that is meant to motivate action. Anyone who takes vengeance against fellow human beings will find God taking vengeance on him because the Lord will refuse to forgive the vengeful person (Sir 28:1). This is set out as a principle from which the wise person should draw the conclusion: Forgive the wrongs done to you by a neighbor, and your sins will be forgiven.

INVESTIGATE

FORGIVE, THAT YOU MIGHT BE FORGIVEN

 Look up the following passages and make notes on the correlation between forgiving and being forgiven.

PASSAGE	NOTES
Matthew 6:12-15	We must forgive others transgressions and them ask God for forgive ours.

Mark 11:25	*When we pray, we have to forgive anyone against whom have a recentiment, then God forgive our sins.*
Luke 17:3	*If our brother sin we all his atention, if he repents, we forgive.*
Ephesians 4:32	*To be kind to one another, patient and forgiving*
Colossians 3:12-13	*When we are in our heart, love is God, help us to be patience, kind gentle, compassion, and forgiven*

CONSIDER

The next part of Sirach's instruction begins with three rhetorical questions (Sir 28:3-5) about harboring anger toward fellow humans while seeking the Lord's healing.

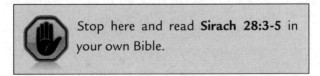

Stop here and read **Sirach 28:3-5** in your own Bible.

The presumed answer to these questions is "Of course not." For our purposes, the second question is worth noting. The person who does not show mercy (Septuagint, *eleos*) toward fellow human beings is wasting his time in praying for his own sins to be forgiven. If someone maintains his wrath against others, it will be impossible to offer a pleasing expiation sacrifice to God. Sacrifices offered in expiation for sin assume that the one making the offering is truly sorry and has changed his mind and attitude regarding sin. However, if he cannot forgive the relatively small sins of the person who offends him, then he can be sure that God will not forgive him either.

 Stop here and read **Sirach 28:6** in your own Bible.

In this verse, Sirach wants the reader to draw some conclusions. First, remember the end of your life; at death, the meaning of life comes together and the truth of the way a person has lived is set before God for his judgment. Second, cease holding enmity toward others, since you will die and be destroyed, ultimately in hell, if you maintain hatred and enmity. Third, keep focused on your own need to keep God's commandments and live a morally straight life. God's judgment will be more thorough than the worries about petty revenge, anger, and enmity against fellow sinners. Instead of trying to avenge their wrongs, make sure you yourself do what is right so as to avoid the absolutely true judgment of God, who will avenge all unforgiveness.

STUDY

Along these very same lines we read an important parable in Matthew 18:21-35 that begins with a question from St. Peter.

 Stop here and read **Matthew 18:21-35** in your own Bible.

The first servant owed his king and master ten thousand talents of gold. A talent was sixty pounds, so his debt was six hundred thousand pounds (not ounces) of gold, worth billions in modern dollars. The second servant owed a hundred denarii, a coin about the size of a half dollar, but made of bronze, about twenty-five dollars' worth of metal in modern value.

Note that each servant petitions his lender for "patience," with a promise to pay the debt. The king goes beyond patience and forgives the enormous debt of gold; the "wicked servant" has no patience and refuses to forgive a small debt. The patience and forgiveness, or the lack thereof, defines "mercy" in Matthew 18:33: the king had mercy, and the wicked servant did not.

CONSIDER

A second group of passages concerns those who are seriously religious but fail to show mercy to sinners who do great evil.

Twice in the Gospel of Matthew Jesus confronts the unwillingness of people to show the acceptance of sinners by quoting Hosea 6:6: "For I desire steadfast love [Hebrew *hesed*; Septuagint *eleos*] and not sacrifice, the knowledge of God, rather than burnt offerings."

The first case occurs in the context of the call of Matthew, the tax collector.

 Stop here and read **Matthew 9:9-11** in your own Bible.

The call of a tax collector was shocking, as seen in Jewish prohibitions of marriage into a family that included a member who was a tax collector. Jesus' next step — going to Matthew's home to share table fellowship with tax collectors and sinners — raised the Pharisees' ire.

Their reaction was partly due to a belief that the Messiah would come only if every member of Israel kept all of God's laws for an hour. Anyone who held that belief understood that the sinners were the people who prevented the arrival of the Messiah.

Jesus responded with a proverbial analogy, followed by the quote from Hosea 6:6.

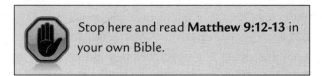

Stop here and read **Matthew 9:12-13** in your own Bible.

First, Jesus speaks a proverb, based on an observation of life that a person of experience can easily accept: Healthy people do not need a physician, but sick people do. Of course, this is long before the very recent practice of visiting a doctor to receive tests for early detection. Physicians were fairly rare and expensive, so the doctor was called only when a person was already sick.

This image of sin as sickness is itself important. Many people emphasize the images of the law court in regard to sin, focusing on which legal precepts were broken, the seriousness of the sin, and the act of justice that makes the sinner right with God again. By comparing sin to sickness, our Lord brings out the aspect of sin's ability to introduce disorder into the sinner's life. The ability to be fully human — that is, someone who fully reflects the image and likeness of God — is impaired and distorted. The juridical and illness models are important complements, along with relational models, for understanding the various aspects of the mystery of evil and sin.

When Jesus moves the Pharisees toward a model of sin as illness and forgiveness as healing, this does not replace the juridical model but complements it, especially as in this case where the sinners have already repented because they are aware of the wrongness of their sin. He cites a higher authority than proverbial wisdom — namely, Scripture: "I desire mercy [*eleos*], and not sacrifice" (Hos 6:6). The point of Jesus' use here is not the rejection of the Old Testament sacrifices as much as it is the desire for mercy to be shown to sinners.

He concludes, "For I came not to call the righteous, but sinners" (Mt 9:13). In complete contrast to the Pharisees' doctrine, Jesus teaches that the sinners do not prevent the coming of the Messiah but instead draw him down. He comes precisely to redeem the sinners. The Pharisees assumed that Israel had to make itself perfect by perfectly obeying the Law in order to deserve the Messiah and his more political redemption of Israel. Jesus is the good Physician, who comes to heal humanity of sin and make people whole.

INVESTIGATE

HEALING AND FORGIVENESS

 Read the following passages and make notes on healing and forgiveness.

PASSAGE	NOTES
Matthew 9:12-13	We pray to God to ill for our sins
Hosea 11:3-4	
Sirach 38:1-15 (especially 9-10, 15)	

STUDY

Another category of ideas about human mercy highlights its inferiority to God's mercy. The first assumption is that humans frequently do not sustain their commitment to principles. History, if not personal experience, shows that people easily exchange the pursuit of a good idea or a noble goal for their own selfish desires. In contrast, God remains focused and does not change, so he can be trusted when people cannot.

A demonstration of this principle occurs in an episode described in 2 Samuel 24 and its parallel in 1 Chronicles 21, wherein David decides to take a census of Israel. The moral problem with this action is that its ultimate purpose was the taxation of the people and the organization of work levies for government projects, as Solomon later did.

The prophet Samuel had warned Israel about seeking a king and a centralized government since a monarch would raise a military draft, work levies, and taxes. Solomon did, in fact, ignore the tribal boundaries and reshape the nation into twelve evenly divided units, for a forced work levy of one month a year from every man for his national building projects. After he died, the people's complaints about this system eventually led to the rebellion of the northern tribes, who formed a new kingdom under Jeroboam I, formerly one of the overseers of the king's forced labor. Such is the background for the sinfulness of David taking the census.

Despite the warnings of his nephew and chief general, Joab, David ordered a census and it was carried out. However, David came to realize that he had done wrong, and the Lord spoke through the prophet Gad to offer three possible punishments to choose from: a three-year famine; three months fleeing his enemies; or three days of plague. David responded to Gad with the words: "I am in great distress; let us fall into the hand of the Lord, for his mercy is great [Hebrew *rabbim rahamo rahamayv*; Septuagint *oiktirmoii autou sphrodos*]; but let me not fall into the hand of man" (2 Sam 24:14). By this saying, David chose the three days of plague, and when the angel of death pointed toward Jerusalem to strike it with plague, David interceded and the Lord relented punishing the people further.

In this episode, David stated the principle that it is better to entrust oneself into the Lord's hand for punishment because one can trust that he is merciful, while humans will not be. In this particular case, after the punishment of the plague had already begun, David's prayer, confession of his own guilt, and his willingness to offer sacrifice opened the way for the Lord's mercy for the people of Jerusalem being spared from the plague. Quite importantly, the location of his prayer became the site of the future Temple, where the rest of the nation would be able to seek the Lord's mercy throughout the coming generations. In other words, the Lord's one act of mercy opens further to many more acts of mercy throughout the subsequent centuries, showing that the Lord's mercy is truly greater than human mercy.

CONSIDER

The same principle appears in an instruction by Sirach, a sage of the early second century B.C. Like most wisdom teachers, he addressed his student as "my son," because his wisdom was a fatherly gift to help a youth understand the inner workings of life. The instruction is a form of speech in which the teacher's wisdom is offered to the students, along with reasons backing it up and exhortations to follow it. This differs from the form of speech known as "proverb," which simply states the results of wise observation of life, leaving it up to the readers to draw their own conclusions about how to act in response to wisdom.

 Stop here and read **Sirach 2:1-18** in your own Bible.

The instruction in Sirach 2 begins with a warning about the good decision to serve the Lord: Whoever does so will be tempted to do evil. Therefore, Sirach exhorts the student to remain steadfast and faithful to the Lord, no matter what may happen, with a promise of honor at the end of life. Just as gold is tested in fire, humiliation tests human beings.

Next, Sirach exhorts the student to trust, hope in, and fear the Lord to receive mercy. He does not describe the mercy for which one should wait but assumes that it is well understood. Sirach then admonishes the student to consider the past history to see if anyone in the past ever trusted in the Lord and was put to shame. Sirach shows a deep familiarity with the history of Israel, as seen in chapters 44-50, so this exhortation is founded upon well-thought-out reflection. His rhetorical questions about trusting in the Lord ever leading to shame is obviously answered in the negative. This is seen in his statement that the Lord is "compassionate and merciful" (Sir 2:11), forgiving sins and saving in affliction.

Sirach continues to motivate faith and trust by warning the student that "woe" will befall those who are timid, slack, sinful, faint-hearted, or lacking in trust or endurance. "Woe" is the term that is opposite "blessing." Those over whom a "woe" is pronounced are already doomed.

On the other hand, Sirach promises those who fear the Lord (one of his fondest values) will move to actual obedience of his words and ways. Fear of the Lord is compatible with love of him, and both lead to seeking his approval and being filled with his law, which is itself the source of real wisdom. Fear of the Lord is also a great good because it leads one to humility.

After all these exhortations, Sirach concludes that we do well to fall into the Lord's hands because his mercy is as great as his majesty — it is infinite. Human mercy may be as high as their majesty, which is not very high. Just as David had prayed after his sin, Sirach concludes that the Lord's mercy is superior to human mercy. However, this comes to him as a result of reflection on the nature of the proper ways to relate to the Lord rather than in the aftermath of punishment for sin, as was the case for David.

DISCUSS

1. What new insights or ideas about the mercy of humans have you learned in this chapter?
2. Why is the image of sin as sickness essential to understanding God's mercy?
3. What is the relationship of forgiveness to mercy?

PRACTICE

This week, consider in what ways you are being called to extend mercy to those around you. If you think of the actions of those who have harmed or offended you as being a "sickness" in need of healing, is it easier or more difficult to extend mercy? Do you think that extending mercy means that you should overlook wrongdoing? Why or why not?

Session 2

WITHHOLDING AND GRANTING MERCY

"Indeed, mercy is the central nucleus of the Gospel message; it is the very name of God, the Face with which he revealed himself in the Old Covenant and fully in Jesus Christ, the incarnation of creative and redemptive Love. May this merciful love also shine on the face of the Church and show itself through the sacraments, in particular that of Reconciliation, and in works of charity, both communitarian and individual. May all that the Church says and does manifest the mercy God feels for man, and therefore for us. When the Church has to recall an unrecognized truth or a betrayed good, she always does so impelled by merciful love, so that men and women may have life and have it abundantly (cf. Jn 10:10). From divine mercy, which brings peace to hearts, genuine peace flows into the world, peace between different peoples, cultures and religions."

— POPE BENEDICT XVI, *Regina Caeli* message on
Divine Mercy Sunday (March 30, 2008)

CONSIDER

A rather difficult and, for many modern people, embarrassing theme in the Bible is God's refusal to show mercy. Not only does he withhold mercy, but he also instructs Israel to do the same. This withholding of mercy stands behind the complete or partial slaughters of Canaanite cities during Israel's conquest of the Promised Land.

Let us look at this withholding of mercy, starting with the sole mention of mercy in the Deuteronomistic history. This occurs in Joshua, in the context of Joshua's campaign against a coalition of city-states led by the large, well-fortified city of Hazor, a very large force that decided to attack the Israelites.

 Stop here and read **Joshua 11:1-20** in your own Bible.

Joshua catches the enemy at Merom and defeats them, chasing them west to the Mediterranean, east to the Jordan valley at Mizpah, and north to Hazor, which he destroys, as confirmed by the archaeology. Joshua is commended for fulfilling the command the Lord had given Moses, with yet another explanation of the reason to destroy the Canaanite in verse 20: "For it was the LORD's doing to harden their hearts that they should come against Israel in battle, in order that they should be utterly destroyed, and should receive no mercy [Hebrew *tehinnah*; Septuagint *eleos*] but be exterminated, as the LORD commanded Moses."

Here, the Hebrew term for "mercy" is derived from the word meaning "be gracious or show favor," which Septuagint translates as simple "mercy."

STUDY

The Book of Wisdom contains a final passage on God withholding mercy and contrasts Egypt, which suffered punishment through the plagues, with Israel, which was tested and disciplined in the wilderness as part of God's mercy.

 Stop here and read **Wisdom 11:1-10** in your own Bible.

The text begins by describing how Wisdom prospered Israel through the "holy prophet" — that is, Moses — as they traveled the desert. The lack of water in the Sinai was an occasion in which the Israelites "called upon" the Lord "and water was given them out of flinty rock, and slaking of thirst from hard stone" (Wis 11:4). Then the author of Wisdom explains that the Egyptians, who were punished by the plague of the Nile water turning to blood, were rebuked for having killed the Israelite boy babies by drowning them in the Nile. The first plague was a fitting punishment for the crime. However, in contrast, Israel was saved by a miracle that used water, when the water came out from a rock and satisfied the people's thirst. He concludes his reflection by saying that the Israelites were being "tested" in the desert in order to discipline them; they were simply being taught and disciplined through their experience of serious thirst in the desert. The "ungodly" Egyptians were judged "in wrath" by God in order to condemn the wickedness of having tried to exterminate Israel (Wis 11:9-10).

INVESTIGATE

FOREIGNERS WHO REFUSE MERCY TO ISRAEL

 Another group of passages relate a number of occasions when foreigners from the great empires refused to extend mercy to Israel.

Look up the following passages and make notes on who refused to extend mercy and what happened to them.

PASSAGE	NOTES
Isaiah 13-23	
Jeremiah 1-6	

STUDY

Jeremiah 46-51 is a series of judgments against the surrounding nations. However, the culmination is his oracles against Babylon in 50-51, which open with the following verses:

> The word which the LORD spoke concerning Babylon, concerning the land of the Chaldeans, by Jeremiah the prophet:
>
> "Declare among the nations and proclaim,
>   set up a banner and proclaim,
>   conceal it not, and say:
> 'Babylon is taken,
>   Bel is put to shame,
>   Merodach is dismayed.

Her images are put to shame,
    her idols are dismayed.' " (Jer 50:1-2)

This threat of destruction against Babylon may have seemed impossible to his hearers, since during Jeremiah's lifetime Babylon was at the height of its power. However, he was proven to have prophesied truly, since Babylon fell to the Persians in October of 539 B.C., just a few decades after Jeremiah's death.

Only one verse mentions mercy: "They lay hold of bow and spear; they are cruel, and have no mercy [Hebrew *velo' yerahamu*; Septuagint *ou me eleesei*]. The sound of them is like the roaring of the sea; they ride upon horses, arrayed as a man for battle against you, O daughter of Babylon!" (Jer 50:42).

DAUGHTER OF ZION

The word "Zion" in the phrase "Daughter of Zion," which refers to Jerusalem, apparently comes from a Hebrew verbal root, *ziyyah*, which means "to be dry." This name is appropriate because looking south and east from ancient Jerusalem, one sees the end of the green and the beginning of the dry desert. The moisture from the Mediterranean Sea is dissipated by the warmer dry winds sweeping up from the Dead Sea and Jordan Valley to the east. Therefore, Zion is the site from which the "dryness" begins.

Originally, this name was applied to the settlement of the Jebusites, a tribe living in the area prior to the Israelites. After David conquered the city and Solomon built the Temple, the name "Zion" was applied specifically to the Temple Mount. After the Romans conquered and destroyed Jerusalem in A.D. 70, they used the Temple Mount for a garbage dump for the next five or six centuries. Meanwhile, Christians returned to Jerusalem in the year 72 and settled near the Upper Room, over which they built a church, and near the house where the Blessed Virgin Mary had "fallen asleep," before the Assumption (formerly called Hagia Sion; today, Dormition Abbey). The Christians renamed this southwestern hill "Mount Zion," and the name is still used for the area to this day.

This is practically the same as Jeremiah 6:22-23, except for one difference: instead of bow and spear being used without mercy against Jerusalem, now they used against Babylon, which had shown Jerusalem no mercy. This clearly is an example of how the one who shows no mercy will be shown no mercy either.

CONSIDER

Another example of withholding mercy comes in Isaiah 40-55, which was written in the late 540s B.C. At the time, the king of Babylon was absent, worshiping the moon god (his mother was an Assyrian priestess of the moon god) in Arabia instead of ruling from Babylon. Meanwhile, Cyrus, the king of Persia, was in the process of conquering the world; first going north of the Babylonian Empire into Media, then Asia Minor, and finally south to Mesopotamia to conquer Babylon in 539 B.C.

While most of Isaiah 40-55 focuses on the Jewish exiles keeping faith with the Lord as the only God, chapters 46-47 speak of the inevitable fall of Babylon as decreed by the Lord.

The key to this oracle is the identification of the Lord of Hosts as the Holy One of Israel and "our Redeemer." He is the one true God who stands behind the oracle (Is 47:4) decreed against the "daughter of the Chaldeans" (that is, Babylon), who had been settled by the Chaldean tribe of Bedouin. Babylon will fall and no longer be "mistress of kingdoms" — that is, ruling over other nations (Is 47:5).

The reason for this judgment was the lack of mercy shown to the Lord's heritage, Israel. The term for mercy, *rahamim*, is the plural form of compassion; the Septuagint, like the English, translates it with the singular form of "mercy" (*eleos*). True, God had declared the punishment of Jerusalem for their sins of worshiping false gods and other crimes. True, the Lord gave Israel into the hands of the Babylonians. However, Babylon was overly enthusiastic in harming Israel and "showed them no mercy" (Is 47:6). The Babylonians even oppressed the aged!

Therefore, the Lord issues his judgment and punishment on the Babylonians. His accusation quotes the Babylonians, who claimed to "be mistress for ever," "there is no one besides me," and the denial of widowhood and loss of children, a reference to military defeat (Is 47:7-8). Babylon did her evil, thinking, "No one sees me" (Is 47:10); however, not only did the Lord see the wicked deeds, but he also noted her arrogance. Therefore, he decrees the punishments: Babylon will be a widow who loses her children — that is, her king and people who will die in the war with the Persians. Evil and disaster will befall her suddenly, and nothing she does will prevent it.

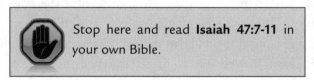

Stop here and read **Isaiah 47:7-11** in your own Bible.

As a result, the message of Isaiah 47:6 is the same as Jeremiah 50:42 — the nation that does not show mercy to the defeated Israel will find no mercy from God.

STUDY

A number of Old Testament passages describe situations in which vulnerable Israelites need the help of powerful leaders. In these situations, they are told to pray to God to move the kings so that he might show mercy to them. The lesson here is that the powerful show mercy when God gives them grace to do so.

The first example is from the time of Jacob and Joseph. Joseph, who was sold as a slave by his ten older brothers, rises to become second-in-command of Egypt. During the great famine, his brothers come to him to buy grain, though they do not recognize him, and he requires them to keep Simeon in Egypt. The famine continues to worsen, as Joseph had predicted, so Jacob agrees to send his sons for more food, even if it means sending Benjamin, Jacob's favorite. At this point, he sends his sons "to the man," whom they do not yet recognize as Joseph, and expresses hope from God, even as he risks bereavement at the possible loss of Benjamin and even his other sons: "Take also your brother, and arise, go again to the man; may God Almighty grant you mercy [*rahamim*; Septuagint *charin*] before the man, that he may send back your other brother and Benjamin. If I am bereaved of my children, I am bereaved" (Gen 43:13-24).

Jacob's short prayer is very insightful. Notice that he prays in a vague way — "may God Almighty grant you mercy before the man." First, only if "the man" (Joseph) shows mercy will the family remain intact. Second, Jacob has no basis for expecting mercy from the man for any human reason; therefore, he turns to God Almighty for help. Third, though this prayer is very early and not theologically well developed, still, it reveals a profound germ of a theology of grace: God is the ultimate source of mercy, and if he pours out graces of mercy on a remote and powerful man in Egypt, then the abundance of that grace might well lead to mercy for the brothers.

EL SHADDAI ("GOD ALMIGHTY")

The English translation in Jacob's prayer uses the name "God Almighty" to translate a Hebrew word, *El Shaddai*. This name first appears in Genesis when God Almighty speaks to Abraham in 17:1, and when Isaac blesses Jacob in 28:3; when God changes Jacob's name to Israel and promises him descendants in 48:3, and in 49:25 when Jacob speaks to Joseph and blesses him. It also appears in Exodus 6:2-3, where God tells Moses: "I am the LORD. I appeared to Abraham, to Isaac, and to Jacob, as God Almighty, but by my name the LORD I did not make myself known to them." This text shows the transition from the older, Mesopotamian name for God to the new name revealed at the burning bush in Exodus 3:14, translated as LORD, or YHWH.

CONSIDER

Another example of coming to the Lord as the source of mercy to be poured out upon powerful rulers occurs in Jeremiah 42.

 Stop here and read **Jeremiah 42:1-10** in your own Bible.

The background is that after the Babylonians had destroyed Jerusalem and had exiled most of the people, a small group of Jewish rebels kill the governor appointed by the Babylonians. The rest of the people still living in the land become afraid of Babylonian revenge and want to flee to Egypt. However, they ask Jeremiah to pray for them about whether they should go to Egypt, and Jeremiah agrees so long as they agree to obey God's word, which they agree to. Ten days later he reveals to them the word that the Lord gave him:

> "If you will remain in this land, then I will build you up and not pull you down; I will plant you, and not pluck you up; for I repent of the evil which I did to you. Do not fear the king of Babylon, of whom you are afraid; do not fear him, says the Lord, for I am with you, to save you and to deliver you from his hand. I will grant you mercy [*rahamim*; Septuagint *eleos*], that he may have mercy [*rahem*; Septuagint *eleeso*] on you and let you remain in your own land." (Jer 42:10-12)

They are to trust the Lord and remain in the land of Judah so that the Lord can build and plant them there. In the context of the Lord's promise, he commands the people not to fear the king of Babylon, Nebuchadnezzar, because the Lord also promises to show mercy to the people so that Nebuchadnezzar might have mercy. This type of compassion (*rahamim*) will be a grace that softens the king's heart to be merciful and not destroy the remainder of the people.

Tragically, the Israelites refuse to believe the word of promise that came through Jeremiah and they flee to Egypt, forcing Jeremiah to go with them. Not too long afterward, King Nebuchadnezzar comes to Egypt with his army and punishes those who had fled there for refuge. This shows that human attempts to avoid danger are not as successful as God's promise of mercy.

CONSIDER

In the middle of the fifth century B.C., Nehemiah, who was the cupbearer to the king of Persia, received a message from Jerusalem that the city was at risk because the walls had not been rebuilt since the time of the Babylonian destruction of the city in 587 B.C. The Persians were not eager to let the Jews rebuild the walls, both because a city wall was an official way to grant a city a certain level of independence and because a walled city might be tempted to revolt against the empire. However, the lack of a wall made the inhabitants vulnerable to raids, particularly by Bedouin nomads, so the people made the request of Nehemiah, the highest Jewish official within the Persian government at that time.

Quite properly, Nehemiah prays, with fasting and tears, to the Lord God before he approaches the king of Persia.

 Stop here and read **Nehemiah 1:1-2:8** in your own Bible.

Nehemiah's address to God — with his qualifiers the "Lord God of heaven" and "great and terrible [that is, 'fearful'] God" — indicates that God is the one who keeps covenant and steadfast love (Neh 1:5). "Steadfast love" is *hesed*, the term for love that exists within a covenant, and which the Septuagint translates as *eleos*, "mercy." This is important to note because a generally recurring theme of mercy in the Bible is that God offers it within the context of the covenantal relationship with Israel.

 Covenant and steadfast love are based on a mutual commitment between God and Israel. However, the history of Israel is one of sin, in which Israel repeatedly breaks the covenant. For that reason, the Lord God, who remains ever faithful to his covenant, adds mercy to the relationship so that he can restore Israel to good standing within the covenant. This is one of the keys to understanding the role of mercy throughout the Bible.

Having established the covenantal love as a basis, Nehemiah asks the Lord to hear his petition, even though Israel has sinned. Next, Nehemiah asks the Lord to remember his promise to gather Israel to his "chosen" place where his "name dwells" — namely, Jerusalem and its Temple — if the people repent and obey his commandments (Neh 1:9).

The key petition concludes the prayer: Grant mercy in the sight of "this man" — namely, the king of Persia — so that God's "servant," Nehemiah, may find success in getting permission to rebuild the walls of Jerusalem (Neh 1:11). Here the terms for "mercy" are *rahamim* and in Septuagint *oiktirmos*, both of which have the nuance of "compassion." As with Jacob's prayer, the assumption is that the Lord God is the source of mercy and compassion, and that he is able to pour this as a gift on a ruler or king, making it possible for him to be merciful.

In fact, Nehemiah 2:1-8 shows that King Artaxerxes already possessed a natural human compassion, as he showed concern and insight into Nehemiah's sadness while serving wine to the king. God's gift of compassion could stir within a heart already open to natural compassion, so Artaxerxes gave Nehemiah permission to go to Jerusalem and rebuild its walls. Nehemiah properly gave the credit for this boon to the "good hand of my God" (Neh 2:8), to whom he had prayed. The rest of the book tells the story of the rebuilding of the walls and gates, the trials and successes, and the impact on the people of Judah. This book is worth reading as the fulfillment of God's mercy and as the fulfillment of the prophecy in Isaiah 60:10, which had been given about thirty years prior to the building of the walls.

STUDY

One last example of prayer for mercy occurs in the first two chapters of the Book of Daniel. Daniel and his three companions had been chosen from among the Jewish exiles in Babylon by King Nebuchadnezzar to take a place among his sages. However, their success in reaching this achievement brought them into a number of dangerous situations throughout the rest of the Book of Daniel.

Daniel 2 explores the situation that occurred when the king had a dream and wanted its interpretation from his court sages. The catch was that he would not tell them his dream, demanding that they demonstrate their ability to interpret by also revealing the dream. If they did so, he would reward them; if they failed, he would kill them all. The Babylonian sages, magicians, and enchanters all despaired of their lives because they did not have such powers of knowledge, nor did their gods.

Daniel asked the king for an appointment in which to interpret the dream. Then he went home to his companions — Hananiah, Mishael, and Azariah — "and told them to seek mercy [*rahamin*] of the God of heaven concerning this mystery, so that Daniel and his companions might not perish with the rest of the wise men of Babylon" (Dan 2:17-18). The Aramaic term for "mercy" here is *rahamin*, a cognate to the Hebrew word for compassion (the Septuagint does not translate this word).

The result of this prayer was that God revealed the "mystery" to Daniel that night, evoking a prayer of praise to God. Then Daniel told the dream and its interpretation to King Nebuchadnezzar, who bowed in homage before Daniel and proclaimed that Daniel's God is "God of gods and Lord of kings, and a revealer of mysteries" (Dan 2:47). Daniel was promoted and the sages were saved by the mercy of God in answer to Daniel's prayer.

DISCUSS

1. What does the Scripture mean when it says that God "hardened" certain people's hearts? Do you think he "hardens hearts" today? Why or why not?
2. What are some of the reasons that God withheld mercy in the Old Testament?
3. What do you see as the relationship between prayer and the granting of mercy? How is this shown by the examples in this chapter?

Prayer is so prayfor

PRACTICE

This week, spend some time reflecting on the different meanings of the words used for "mercy" in the Scriptures. How are they similar and how are they different? What ways have you experienced these aspects of mercy in your own life?

- *Rahamim,* a term derived from the Hebrew word for "womb." The womb is an all-encompassing reality for a baby, and that is one of the most common terms for mercy in the Old Testament.
- *Oiktirei,* meaning "have compassion." *soft heart*
- *Hanan,* meaning to "be gracious," or "show grace or favor."
- *Tehinnah,* meaning "supplication."
  pray for people

Session 3

AN OVERVIEW OF GOD'S MERCY

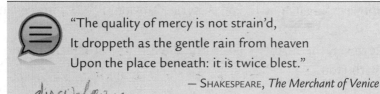

"The quality of mercy is not strain'd,
It droppeth as the gentle rain from heaven
Upon the place beneath: it is twice blest."

— SHAKESPEARE, *The Merchant of Venice*

discipline

The religions of the great civilizations that surrounded the Holy Land developed in warm-weather regions around good water sources — the Nile, the Tigris and Euphrates, the Orontes. The religious stories of these ancient civilizations take the form of myths about deities who determined the shape of their world before human history began. Predominantly, the gods were the personifications of the forces of nature — fresh water, salt water, the wind, the sun, the moon, the sea, the storm, and even death. Through various sexual liaisons and battles, they established the world and made human beings. History was primarily the stories of their kings and their reigns and conquests.

The religion of Israel, on the other hand, is historically, not mythologically oriented. In Israel, history begins with the creation of the world and humanity, with no description of God prior to creation. God creates the forces of nature, but he is not one of them; no other deities exist but God, and the forces of nature are simply creatures. The focus is on God's ways of relating to the creature that crowns the six days of making good creatures: humanity, which is not merely good but is made in God's image and likeness as persons who are "very good" (Gen 1:27, 31).

However, this relationship has its own difficulties, as humans choose to disobey God's commandments, from the very simplest to the most complex. Certainly, the history of the human race, and of Israel in particular, is portrayed as one of societal and cultural growth. Humanity had to learn to develop its skills, and Israel itself experienced a long development from a simple semi-nomadic existence to a fairly well-developed Iron Age complex civilization living between superpowers — such as Egypt, Assyria, Babylon, Persia, Greece, and Rome.

However, the history told in the Bible is one of Israel's relationship with God.

STUDY

We now turn to six prophetic texts that illustrate the history of Israel's relationship with God.

Hosea

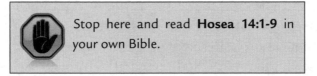
Stop here and read **Hosea 14:1-9** in your own Bible.

Recall that the prophet Hosea exercised his ministry in northern Israel from about the 750s B.C., soon after the prophetic ministry of Amos. He criticized the people of the Northern Kingdom for their many sins, which included the fashioning of two golden calf idols — one at Dan and the other at Bethel. Throughout the first 13 chapters of his book, he threatens Israel with punishment for its many infractions of the Ten Commandments, including idolatry and the worship of the golden calves in Dan and Bethel. However, Hosea 14 offers some hope of reconciliation after the Israelites had "stumbled" by committing iniquity.

Habakkuk

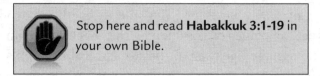
Stop here and read **Habakkuk 3:1-19** in your own Bible.

This whole passage is "a prayer of Habakkuk the prophet," which is meant to be sung, as indicated by two musical instructions: "according to Shigionoth" (Hab 3:1), which was the name of a well-known melody, now lost to us; and in 3:19b he says, "To the choirmaster: with stringed instruments." Perhaps Habakkuk was a priest, or more likely a Levite, who belonged to the Temple staff and was accustomed to leading the people in hymns as well as being a prophet. This chapter is a hymn with different movements that are distinguished according to the one being addressed or the manner of address.

Habakkuk opens the hymn with a direct address to the Lord that expresses faith in what the Lord has done in the past and then requests him to renew his saving actions in the present. Note that he makes a statement of faith that he not only knows the Lord's past deeds, but he also has "fear" of them — a way of expressing proper respect for the almighty Lord God. Based on that faith and proper respect, he petitions the Lord to renew these deeds and make them known again. Even though he is angry for his people's sins, Habakkuk asks God to remember mercy even in the midst of his wrath.

Next, Habakkuk gives a report of the history of God's past deeds, speaking of God in the third person. This section refers to the primary act of God's salvation: He met Moses in the desert of Sinai (the general location of Teman and Mount Paran), and sent plagues to Egypt in order to free Israel from slavery.

Then Habakkuk gives a personal testimony to having seen the tents of the enemies shake in fear. The precise events are not known, but the people hearing this hymn could relate to it.

Next, Habakkuk addresses the Lord in a prayer that begins with rhetorical questions about whether the real objects of the Lord's wrath were the creatures of nature, such as the rivers, sea, or mountains. It is useful to remember that the pagans had deified all of these creatures and worshiped the Nile River, the sea god (called Yam by the Canaanites or Poseidon by the Greeks), the sun, and the moon. The assumed answer of these rhetorical questions is "No." Israel understood all of these elements of nature as mere creatures that are morally neutral and therefore incapable of either sin or virtue; they just follow the course that belongs to their nature.

However, the direct address to the Lord continues when Habakkuk identifies the real objects of the Lord's fury as the enemy nations so that the Lord might save his people Israel and their anointed king.

In conclusion, Habakkuk sets forth his personal response of complete faith in the Lord, no matter how grim and impossible the situation may seem. During his prophetic ministry, Israel was in a very precarious position. Their former Assyrian enemies and oppressors were in the process of being completely defeated by the Babylonians and Medes. However, the Babylonians were subsequently on the march to conquer the same extent of empire as the Assyrians, thereby including Egypt and Israel (the latter through which they had to march in order to get to Egypt).

The amazing component of Habakkuk's faith is that he sees "the day of trouble" (Hab 3:16) coming as the Babylonians approach Judah, and he is aware that the crops and herds are failing to provide food. Yet, by faith he does not merely hang in with raw belief but rather he rejoices in the Lord God of salvation. Beyond simply expressing ideas of faith, his trust in God is expressed in praise and joy. For that reason verse 19 is yet another statement of faith in God as his strength: "God, the Lord, is my strength; he makes my feet like hinds' feet, he makes me tread upon my high places."

Habakkuk believes that the mercy for which he prayed at the beginning of this hymn will give him a strength that an abundance of food cannot. This hymn is a wonderful expression of the link between faith — a faith that can perceive the Lord acting even in the midst of surrounding disasters — and God remembering his mercy.

Jeremiah

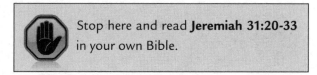
Stop here and read **Jeremiah 31:20-33** in your own Bible.

Jeremiah, a prophet from a family of priests, began his critique of Judah by 627 B.C. His warnings to Judean society were very strong, but it seems that King Josiah paid attention, as witnessed by the reforms of the nation's faith life. However, when Josiah died in battle at Megiddo, his foolish sons were unable to sustain the reforms or keep the nation politically stable. Jeremiah began the second phase of his career, warning the kings and the people of the Lord's coming punishment for their sins, until the disaster of the destruction of Jerusalem and its Temple by the Babylonians, with the subsequent exile of the people to Babylon.

However, Jeremiah did not say, "I told you so." Rather, his oracles after this catastrophe offered hope and comfort, including a promise of mercy. Both the Hebrew and the Greek literally say, "I will mercifully have mercy," translated well into English as "surely I will have mercy" (cf. Jer 31:20). This is a Hebrew form of speech to emphasize how merciful the Lord will be in showing mercy after the people have experienced the devastating punishment of exile. In fact, a few verses later the Lord promises that the days will come when the Lord will make a new covenant with his people.

Recall that the Lord's promise of mercy to Moses is connected with the Lord's promise to remain present with the people and then renew the covenant. So also here, in Jeremiah, the promise to "surely be merciful" precedes the promise of a new covenant within the hearts of the people and the maintenance of the Lord's relationship of being "their God" and they being "my people" (Jer 31:33). The rest of the Old Testament fails to mention the actualization of this "new covenant," but at the Last Supper Jesus says it is fulfilled when he says, "This cup is the new covenant in my blood" (1 Cor 11:25).

Ezekiel

 Stop here and read **Ezekiel 39:25, 37:1-27** in your own Bible.

Ezekiel is yet another priest who received the prophetic call. He had been taken to Babylon, in the first deportation, by the Babylonian king Nebuchadnezzar in 598 B.C., along with King Jehoiachin, military leaders, and artisans. While living in Babylon, Ezekiel received his prophetic call and warned the people that Jerusalem would be destroyed, exactly as Jeremiah was doing back in Jerusalem throughout this period of the 590s. Once Jerusalem was destroyed, he also, like Jeremiah, did not say, "I told you so," but he also gave oracles of hope that the Lord God would restore Judah. In that context, we read the promise of mercy in Ezekiel 39:25. This promise of mercy is likewise connected with a promise of a new covenant and the Lord's presence with his people.

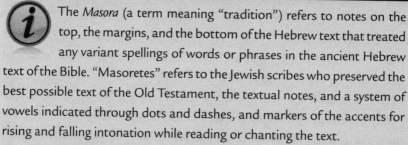

THE MASORETIC TEXT (MT)

The *Masora* (a term meaning "tradition") refers to notes on the top, the margins, and the bottom of the Hebrew text that treated any variant spellings of words or phrases in the ancient Hebrew text of the Bible. "Masoretes" refers to the Jewish scribes who preserved the best possible text of the Old Testament, the textual notes, and a system of vowels indicated through dots and dashes, and markers of the accents for rising and falling intonation while reading or chanting the text.

Three different schools of Masoretes existed: Palestinian (fifth century A.D.), Babylonian, and the Ben Asher school in Tiberias (tenth century A.D.), which became the final and authoritative school still used by the Jewish communities around the world. Their earliest known copy of the Old Testament dates to ca. 925 and is known as the Masoretic Text (MT). It remains the starting point for Scripture scholars studying the Old Testaments, whether Jewish or Christian.

In Ezekiel 37, the Lord promises to raise the dead and restore them to life and to reunite the two kingdoms of Israel and Judah into one, with a descendant of David as their ruler. At that point, the Lord then promises a new covenant and his intimate presence with the people: That promise of renewal is followed in Ezekiel 38-39 by a promise to destroy the evil enemies of the nation, and finally he speaks of mercy in 39:25: "Therefore thus says the Lord GOD: Now I will restore the fortunes of Jacob, and have mercy [MT *rahamti*; Septuagint *eleeso*] upon the whole house of Israel; and I will be jealous for my holy name."

Zechariah

 Stop here and read **Zechariah 1:12-17** and **Jeremiah 25:11; 29:10-14** in your own Bible.

Zechariah is prophesying in Jerusalem after the first groups of Jews returned from Babylon to Jerusalem, beginning in 539 B.C., when Cyrus, the king of the Persians, let the Jews return home. After Cyrus died childless, a dynastic struggle took place in Persia in 522 B.C., with Darius coming out the new king. In 520 B.C., both the prophet Haggai and the prophet Zechariah began their ministry of preaching the word of the Lord that instructed the people to rebuild the Temple. The returning exiles had begun to rebuild the Temple in 539, but then they stopped work in order to build their own homes and farms. In 520, the prophets ordered them to finish the Temple, since worshiping the Lord was the most central issue of their existence as God's chosen people.

Zechariah experienced the angel of the Lord as the mediator between him and the Lord, instructing him about the various visions he sees. Within this relationship with the angel of the Lord, he sees the angel interceding for the nation: "Then the angel of the LORD said, "O LORD of hosts, how long will you have no mercy [MT *terahem*; Septuagint *eleeseis*] on Jerusalem and the cities of Judah, against which you have had indignation these seventy years?" (Zech 1:12, RSV-SCE). (The seventy years of suffering had been prophesied twice by Jeremiah in 25:11 and 29:10-14.)

Now that it is over, the angel of the Lord prays to know "how long will you have no mercy?" This is a rhetorical device that means, "Lord, it is time to show mercy," since the prescribed time of the punishment is complete. The Lord answers favorably in Zechariah 1:13-17. The word translated as "compassion" in 1:16 is *rehamim*, a plural noun derived from the verb used in 1:12 to mean "show mercy." Therefore, it is a direct answer to the angel's request for mercy upon Judah at the end of the prescribed seventy years of punishment.

As has been the case with the previous passages from Exodus and the prophets, mercy is bestowed after punishment for the people's sin and infidelity to the Lord. This passage, as with the above, also includes a promise to rebuild the house of the Lord — that is, the Temple, where the people can approach the presence of the Lord. Consistently, mercy is not just a vague gift of reconciliation, but it also includes renewed intimacy with the presence of the Lord.

Isaiah

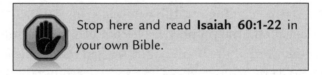

Stop here and read **Isaiah 60:1-22** in your own Bible.

These verses in Isaiah are a proclamation of salvation, that the Lord's presence in Jerusalem will be the sole light in the world's darkness that draws all people there. The effects of the Lord's light will cause Israel to be radiant and rejoice, and the nations will stream toward this sole light. Verses 10-16 form a description of salvation focused on the rebuilding and beautification of the city of Jerusalem. The Babylonians destroyed Jerusalem in 587 B.C. and dismantled the walls to prevent further revolts. When the people returned in 539 B.C., the Persians did not give them permission to rebuild the walls, which left them vulnerable to attack and living in fear.

THE CANON OF THE OLD TESTAMENT

The canon of the Old Testament has been a matter of dispute for millennia and remains so, due to differences of principles for canonicity within each religious community. All Jews consider the Torah, or Pentateuch (the first five books of the Bible), the sacred word of God. Differences among the Jewish sects arose by the second century B.C., with Sadducees (the priests and the nobles) limiting the canon to the Torah; with the Pharisees and Essenes including the prophets and other writings in the canon, though without clearly stating its precise limits; and with Diaspora Jews, particularly in Alexandria, Egypt, continuing to accept and translate a number of books into Greek, as well as compose two new ones in Greek — namely, 2 Maccabees and the Book of Wisdom.

After the destruction of the Temple by the Romans in A.D. 70, the Essenes and Sadducees were wiped out, so their canonical concerns became irrelevant. The Pharisees finished their refinement of the limits of the canon in the early second century, with the guidance of Rabbi Akiba, resulting in thirty-nine books in their canon. Their decisions became authoritative for the rest of the Jews, including those living in the Diaspora.

Alexandria, Egypt

Alexander the Great established Alexandria (one of many cities he named after himself) as a Mediterranean port for Egypt and as a center for spreading Greek culture. The city was famous for its schools and especially for its library. Jews were moved to settle the new city before 300 B.C., and they flourished as a vibrant, large population, both economically and intellectually, eventually producing the great scholar Philo in the first century A.D. The Bible was translated into Greek at Alexandria, beginning around 250 B.C., with the Pentateuch, and the rest of the Old Testament was translated over the next hundred or more years. This was the Septuagint (LXX) that was cited in the New Testament over three hundred times and is still consulted by scholars today.

The Lord explains that even though he had punished them with the destruction of the whole city, as he had warned, still he has now decided to show them mercy: his wrath gives way to mercy, as in earlier passages. (This text probably belongs to the early 400s; in fact, based on the announcement of a Jubilee in 61:1-3, it would be in 473 B.C.)

Isaiah 60:10 announces that foreigners will rebuild the walls of Jerusalem. In fact, Nehemiah felt called to come from Persia, where he had been born, to Jerusalem in 444 B.C., to rebuild the walls. He received permission from Persian King Artaxerxes I to build the walls thirty years after this prophecy.

STUDY

The Deuterocanonical books Judith and Tobit are an important source for the study of mercy in Scripture. They contain a continuity of thought between the earlier Old Testament books and the developments toward the New Testament uses of the terms for mercy. They will also prove interesting because the uses of mercy are more concentrated in these books than in any one other section of the Bible.

The Book of Judith

The Book of Judith treats a time of extreme crisis for the Israelites after their return from exile. The story speaks of Nebuchadnezzar waging a war against the Persians, in which he requires all of his subject peoples to join him. He defeats the Persians without them but then sends his chief general, Holofernes, to destroy all the people who refused to join his campaign, to preclude any future rebellions. After successful campaigns against various nations, the story focuses on Israel, whose primary strategy centers on the defense of narrow passes into the country. A central part of this story is Holofernes' council before attacking Israel. An Ammonite leader, Achior, advises him on strategy but warns him that if the people have pleased God by obeying him, then any attack is futile. He backs up his claim with a summary of the history of Israel succeeding when they have faith and experiencing defeat when they sin. Holofernes threatens him with death and sends him to the Israelite city of Bethulia in order to die with its defenders.

In the face of the overwhelming army of Holofernes encamped near the Israelite city of Bethulia, and with the Assyrian army capturing all the springs of water, the townspeople cry out in despair against the town council led by Uzziah (whose name means "Strength of the Lord"). The people accuse their leaders of foolishly trying to resist the invaders, and they prefer surrender over dying of thirst. In their despair they say, "For now we have no one to help us; God has sold us into their hands" (Jud 7:25), and "We call to witness against you heaven and earth and our God, the Lord of our fathers, who punishes us according to our sins and the sins of our fathers. Let him not do this day the things which we have described!" (Jud 7:28).

In response to their lament, Uzziah answers with a faith that leads him to have hope in God's mercy:

"Have courage, my brothers! Let us hold out for five more days; by that time the Lord our God will restore to us his mercy, for he will not forsake us utterly. But if these days pass by, and no help comes for us, I will do what you say." (Jud 7:30-31)

At this point the book introduces the heroine, Judith, a beautiful and wise woman who was widowed a few years prior. Speaking to the city council, she poignantly upbraids them for setting a five-day limit before surrender as a lack of faith. Judith tells the council to trust her, though she does not trust them enough to tell them her plans, but she prays to God for help. She goes out to the enemy camp with an offer to help them take the city of Bethulia without losing a man. The soldiers are awed by her beauty, and so is Holofernes. He makes her a guest and desires to sleep with her after a banquet in which much wine is drunk. After all his servants are dismissed to give them privacy, Holofernes falls asleep from too much wine, and she, in her sobriety, cuts off his head and hands it to her maid, who stuffs it into a bag, and they walk peacefully out of camp (which Judith had made her nightly custom), bringing the head to Bethulia. At this point, she loudly praises God before her people.

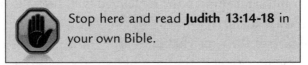

Stop here and read **Judith 13:14-18** in
your own Bible.

INVESTIGATE

WOMEN'S SONGS OF VICTORY

During the victory celebration, Judith leads the people in a victory song. Look up the following passages and compare the hymns of Miriam, Deborah, and the women's song about David and Saul to Judith's victory song. Which elements are common to them and which are distinctive in each? What does this say about the role of ancient women in victorious situations? Note that Judith's song refers to mercy.

PASSAGE	NOTES
Judith 16:1-17	16} 14:15 Those who fear the Lord he show his mercy
Exodus 15:20-21	The prophetess Miriam, Aaron's sister, took a tambourim in her hand all the women went on after dancing and singing in the refrain sing to the Lord ! for he is gloriously
Judges 5	triumphant; horse and chariots he has cast into the sea
1 Samuel 18:7-8	when David return after slaying the Philistine, the women came to meet King Saul singing and dancing; They play and sing Saul has slain his thousands and David his 10 thousands

Book of Wisdom

The Book of Wisdom (or The Wisdom of Solomon), written in Greek in Alexandria, Egypt, confronts a number of issues that were posed by various pagans who were criticizing Judaism. Many of these issues were philosophical, and others were criticisms of Israel's historical claims to be God's chosen people. This was a particularly sensitive issue in Egypt, the place from which God had delivered the people of Israel through devastating plagues. For instance, the Egyptian priest and historian Manetho (who divided Egyptian history into the structure of dynasties that is still used today), who lived about two hundred years before Wisdom was written, claimed that Israel was driven out of Egypt because they had a disease. That, and presumably other criticisms, helped provoke the writing of this Book of Wisdom, apparently in the first century B.C. We will examine the role of mercy in author's defense of God's treatment of the Egyptians at the Exodus and the Canaanites in the Promised Land.

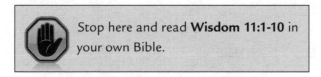

Stop here and read **Wisdom 11:1-10** in your own Bible.

An important manifestation of God's wisdom came through "the hand of a holy prophet" (Wis 11:1) — namely, Moses. This author points out that water is the backdrop for a number of events for good and for evil. Because the Egyptians drowned the boy children of the Hebrews, Moses stretched out his staff over the same Nile River and turned it to blood. Later, the Egyptians went against their promise to let Israel leave, and they were punished by being drowned in the sea. However, the Israelites, who ran out of water in the desert, experienced the miracle of Moses striking the rock with the same staff and causing water to flow out.

The explanation of these contrasts between punishment and salvation through the same element of water is that Israel was being disciplined in mercy and tested the way a father warns a child. However, the Egyptians were tormented as the Lord judged them in his wrath, similar to the way a stern king acts toward the condemned. In this way, the text shows that God's mercy and wrath coexist, and the wise person learns to accept the discipline as a sign of mercy and avoid the wrath.

INVESTIGATE

GOD'S "TOUGH LOVE"

The teaching in Wisdom 11 may at first seem strange to modern ears, but that may say more about the fear of the modern world to discipline people as a way to morally improve them. Being tough in discipline is not so highly prized in modern society as it was in past times. The proverbs about the necessity of disciplining a child are disregarded and even feared, since the state often intervenes when parents use corporal discipline.

Look up the following passages and make notes on God's view about discipline.

PASSAGE	NOTES
Proverbs 19:18	*Chastise your son, for in this there is hope. But no desire his death*
John 15:1-2	*Endure our trials, and obey the Lord*
Hebrews 12:7-11	

60

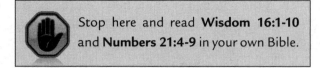

Stop here and read **Wisdom 16:1-10** and **Numbers 21:4-9** in your own Bible.

The passage from Wisdom 16 returns to the same theme as Wisdom 11: while Egypt experienced an unremitting punishment through animals throughout the plagues, in the wilderness Israel experienced the presence of wild animals as a kindness or a punishment, followed by God showing them mercy.

The first contrast is that the Egyptians received a just punishment for their sins of enslaving Israel and then trying to kill all of the Israelites' male children. However, Israel, which was freed from Egypt by the ten plagues, went into the Sinai desert and received the "kindness" (Wis 16:2) of eating quails, a delicacy that was not available to the Israelites during their time of enslavement. This treat during Israel's newly found freedom highlighted the contrast between them and the Egyptians, who were tormented by plagues through various nasty animals, such as frogs, gnats, and flies.

The second contrast, in Numbers 21, refers to the punishment of Israel in the wilderness through "seraph" or "fiery serpents." They complained about eating manna, calling it "worthless food," after having eaten it for thirty-nine years of desert wandering. The Lord punished their ingratitude through serpents whose bite was "fiery" to them, and some of them died. However, Wisdom 16:6 says this was a "warning" to them, and Number 21:7 describes their words of repentance: "We have sinned, for we have spoken against the LORD and against you; pray to the LORD, that he take away the serpents from us." In response to Moses' prayer, the Lord instructed him to make a serpent out of bronze and hang it on a pole, so that anyone who looked at it after a snakebite would be healed. This bronze serpent was the "token of deliverance" that reminded them of the "law's command" (Wis 16:6).

Wisdom adds an important theological point here: the people who looked at the bronze serpent were not healed by some power in that molten image, but by the Lord, who is "the Savior of all"

(Wis 16:7). Then the contrast is made between the Egyptians, who were bitten by locusts and flies, who found nothing that could offer them relief or healing, and Israel, which was not defeated by the venomous serpents. Again the text emphasizes that the Egyptians deserved their punishment. However, the Israelites are the Lord's "sons," who receive his mercy in the form of help and healing. This understanding of the term "mercy" here contributes to the Gospel use of mercy in reference to healings and exorcisms.

INVESTIGATE

LIFTING UP THE SON OF MAN

Numbers 21:4-9 relates the episode of the bronze serpent. Jesus refers to the bronze serpent once, in John 3:14-17.

Read these passages and consider the following question: What is the image Jesus is describing here by comparing the lifting up of the Son of Man to the bronze serpent?

A hint is that the bronze serpent was an image of a snake stretched out: while a coiled snake would be an image of an aggressive serpent about to strike someone, a stretched-out snake is one that is fleeing. Picture that bronze serpent placed on a pole, and then picture what Jesus is describing. If looking at the bronze serpent with faith could heal the Israelites of serpent bites, what does faith in the lifted-up Son of Man heal?

PASSAGE	NOTES
Numbers 21:4-9	
John 3:14-17	

A third passage in Wisdom that mentions mercy is yet another contrast between Israel and pagans. However, instead of a contrast with the Egyptians, this is a contrast with the Canaanites.

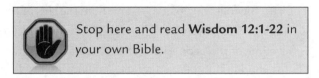

Stop here and read **Wisdom 12:1-22** in your own Bible.

The opening verses (Wis 12:1-2) establish two basic principles that guide the rest of the text. First, God places his immortal spirit within human beings. The presence of an immortal spirit is what gives people their great value in God's estimation; humans are not mere things to be disregarded but instead are precious, undying creatures that God wants to be holy for all eternity.

Second, though these immortal souls sin and commit trespasses, the Lord corrects them little by little so as to help them to be freed from wickedness and to put their trust in God. He is willing to take all the steps necessary to make them holy as individuals and as societies.

The next section describes the wickedness of the peoples who lived in the land of Canaan and the Lord's willingness to try and improve them over time. The primary sins for which he condemned them were sorcery, magic, and human sacrifices.

Certainly the Lord had sent the ancient Israelites to punish the Canaanites who had done these terrible crimes in the land identified as God's "holy land" that is "most precious." Yet, even many of these Canaanites were spared because the Lord understood that they were mere human beings in need of various chances to repent; their punishment was gradual and "little by little" so that they might have opportunities to repent of their wickedness. However, they did not change their ways, and they were eventually dispossessed of their land by the Israelites.

INVESTIGATE

 Look up the following passages and note the sins of the Canaanites for which they were being expelled from the land. ("Amorites" is the name of the people who settled Canaan in Abram's time.)

PASSAGE	NOTES
Genesis 15:16	
Leviticus 18:24-30	
Deuteronomy 9:1-5	
Deuteronomy 12:29-31	
Deuteronomy 18:9-12	

CONSIDER

Many modern people not only question God's right to punish the Canaanite people but even use it as a reason not to believe in God at all — he is far too cruel in allowing their deaths, and no one that mean can be a good God.

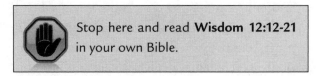

Stop here and read **Wisdom 12:12-21** in your own Bible.

These verses from the Book of Wisdom present a series of arguments against that type of reasoning, which was apparently the logic used by some of the Greek-speaking pagans of Alexandria, Egypt, in the first century B.C., who also disliked the Lord as some moderns do.

Some points that are covered include these:

- Rhetorical questions concerning the ability to judge what God has done by punishing the wicked, or to resist his judgment, or to accuse him of having been wrong in destroying those wicked nations, or to even plead the case for the unrighteous — the presumed answer is "no one" can resist this judgment.

- Neither the gods nor human rulers have any grounds for condemning God for having punished the Canaanites. The pagan gods were local deities who cared only for a particular people or were specialists in charge of only one arena of the universe — for example, the sun god, moon god, storm god, sea god, etc. However, the Lord God of Israel has care for all people and the whole universe, since he alone created everything, and the sun, moon, sea, etc., are not deities but merely his creatures. Therefore, these mere creatures have no basis for accusing the Lord for judging the Canaanites unjustly.

- Righteousness is inherent in God. He is righteous and rules the universe righteously. It is contrary to his nature to condemn the innocent person who does not deserve punishment. While various tyrannical human beings use their raw power to execute their will, even with evil intent, the divine power wielded by God is the source of his righteousness. If anything, his sovereignty leads God to "spare all" (Wis 12:16). This is manifested by his shows of strength when people doubt that his power is complete or when he rebukes the insolent. Since all people are sinners who doubt him, act insolently, and disobey him, the very fact that all people are not totally destroyed is evidence that the Lord is forbearing in sparing people the full punishment they deserve.

- God is the Lord who is sovereign in strength toward Israel, as he was toward the Canaanites, capable of manifesting power whenever he chooses. However, his powerful deeds have taught Israel that righteousness includes kindness, as seen when the Lord bestows repentance for sins. That gift of repentance is itself a reason for believers to have hope in God.

- The Lord showed "great care and indulgence" when he punished the Canaanite enemies, who were deserving of death for their crimes; he delayed in punishment for a long time so that they might have an opportunity to "give up their wickedness" (Wis 12:20). Yet, the Lord has been strict in judging the people of Israel, who have received his covenants (with Abraham, at Mount Sinai, and with David), which contain great promises of blessing for those who keep the commandments contained in those covenants.

The believers are expected to draw two conclusions from all this. First, Israel's enemies are punished far worse than the people of faith so that believers may meditate on God's goodness. Second, when believers are judged by God, they can examine his dealings with the Canaanites and learn to expect mercy.

DISCUSS

1. What are some of the key points regarding God's relationship with Israel and his mercy that you have noted in this chapter?
2. If God is considered "all-merciful," how can he also be judgmental and punishing?
3. What is one lesson that you have learned from the book of Judith and her great song of thanksgiving and praise?

PRACTICE

Think about the times you have personally experienced God's mercy in your life. What was your reaction? Now consider times when God may have been rebuking you. What was your reaction? Spend some time reflecting on how God's mercy and his judgment always go together.

Session 4

MERCY AND COVENANT LOVE

> "In this way, in Christ and through Christ, God also becomes especially visible in His mercy; that is to say, there is emphasized that attribute of the divinity which the Old Testament, using various concepts and terms, already defined as 'mercy.' Christ confers on the whole of the Old Testament tradition about God's mercy a definitive meaning. Not only does He speak of it and explain it by the use of comparisons and parables, but above all He Himself makes it incarnate and personifies it. He Himself, in a certain sense, is mercy. To the person who sees it in Him — and finds it in Him — God becomes 'visible' in a particular way as the Father 'who is rich in mercy' (Eph 2:4)."
>
> — POPE ST. JOHN PAUL II, *Dives in Misericordia* (n. 2)

A strong link exists between mercy and covenant love. Many scholars over the years have pointed out that the Israelite understanding of mercy is strongly tied into their understanding of a covenant relationship with the Lord. Covenants were well known in the ancient Near East, as evidenced by a number of treaties between various nations. These covenants were usually made between a greater king, or suzerain, and lesser kings, who were their vassals. A few covenants existed between equals, such as between the Hittite Empire and Egypt, but most covenants defined the relationships between suzerains and vassals, usually at the instigation of the suzerain, who threatened to destroy the weaker kings who did not accept the covenant.

Commonly, the form of these covenants began with the great king or suzerain giving his name and listing his titles, followed by a history of his benefits to the vassal. Then came the stipulations of the covenant, spelling out the obligations each party had to the other. Usually a list of punishments for noncompliance or rewards for fidelity to the covenant were included, along with a list of witnesses to the covenant, typically the local deities or even the mountains, rivers, and other natural phenomena that the people could expect to outlive the signers of the treaty, with a description of the place where the treaty would be kept and read on a regular basis.

INVESTIGATE

COVENANTS: THE DETAILS

Most of these elements of the covenant treaty can be found within the Pentateuch, though not entirely within a single passage.

Look up the following passage and note the name, title, history of past benefits and stipulations, punishments or rewards.

• Exodus 20:1-17	*The ten Commandments*

Look up the following passages and note description of the depository of the covenant.

• Exodus 25:10-26:37	*Contribution, gold, silver, bronze, violet, purple and scarlet yarn. Make an Ark of acacia wood*

• Deuteronomy 27:1-10	
• Exodus 21-23; 34	
• Deuteronomy 12-26	

Look up the following passage and note rewards for compliance and punishments for disobedience.

• Deuteronomy 27-28	

Look up the following passages and note the regulation for reading of the covenant.

• Deuteronomy 31:9-13	

• Joshua 8:34-35	
• 2 Kings 23:1-3	
• Nehemiah 8	

STUDY

The covenant was most important in establishing a relationship between two parties. This clearly differs from a mere contract, which establishes an agreement for providing services or goods and payment between two parties. However, rendering the services or goods does not establish an enduring relationship. For instance, with a contract, one may hire a cook for a certain amount of money and a prescribed time of employment. In distinction, when a man and woman marry, they cook for each other for the rest of their lives, but only because they have established a permanent bond within which services like cooking might occur. Even when neither can cook for each other, the marital bond remains until death do them part.

This helps us better understand the covenant that the Lord made with Israel: the covenant established a relationship between them, defined by the statement, "I will be your God, and you shall be my people" (Jer 7:23). Within the scope of the relationship, the stipulations of the covenant have their meaning.

Another consideration of the types of covenants is useful for understanding the history of covenants in the Bible. One kind of covenant is unconditional, while other covenants are conditional. In the unconditional covenants, God commits himself without stipulating any particular human behavior. A conditional covenant sets out the stipulations that people must fulfill in order to receive the promises God offers. The unconditional covenants were made with Noah, Abraham, and David; the conditional covenant is at Mount Sinai.

INVESTIGATE

COVENANTS: UNCONDITIONAL AND CONDITIONAL

 Look up the following passages and note the ways that they convey unconditional covenants.

• Genesis 9	Noah and his sons unconditional
• Genesis 12:1-3	Abraham conditional covenants
• Genesis 15:1-19 (the smoking brazier, or fire pot, symbolizes God's presence)	It was on that occasion that the made a covenant with Abram conditional
• 2 Samuel 7	David concern for the ark unconditional

Look up the following passages and consider the indications of the conditional nature of the Sinai Covenant.

• Exodus 19:5-6	*Keep god covenant*
• Exodus 23:22-23	*Fidelity*
• Leviticus 26	*Obedience*
• Numbers 14:6-9	*Treat revolt*
• Deuteronomy 8:19-20	*Forget the Lord and follow other idols*
• Deuteronomy 11:13-32; 30 (especially verses 15-18)	

CONSIDER

The issue of mercy becomes relevant when the Israelites transgress the conditions of the covenant with God. By breaking his commandments, which are the stipulations of the covenant, they set themselves up for exclusion from the covenantal relationship and its promises. Throughout their history, they experience this exclusion from the covenant by means of defeats by enemies, plagues, famines, droughts, and other natural disasters. In fact, the writers of Judges through Kings and Chronicles try to show that breaking the commandments leads to punishment, including the catastrophic exiles in 722 B.C., when the Assyrians defeated the northern Kingdom of Israel, and in 587 B.C., when the Babylonians destroyed Jerusalem and exiled the people.

However, the Lord also extends mercy to individuals and to the people of Israel as a nation. In fact, the reason he shows the people mercy is because he remains faithful to the covenantal relationship, even when they become unfaithful. That fidelity to the covenant makes possible *hesed*, which, as we have seen, is a Hebrew word derived from a root meaning "to be kind."

Hesed designates a particular type of love — the love to which one is committed when in a covenantal relationship. Another Hebrew

PENTATEUCH AND TORAH

Pentateuch is the Greek term for the Torah — that is, the first five books of the Bible: Genesis, Exodus, Leviticus, Numbers, and Deuteronomy. *Torah* is a Hebrew word meaning "instruction," though many people call it the "Law," following the tradition of the Jews who lived among the Greeks, since they could point to the Torah as the source of their 613 binding laws. St. Paul, a Jew who had been born in the Greek-speaking city of Tarsus, also refers to the Pentateuch as the Law, thereby influencing many Christians. Yet, Torah, or "instruction," is more accurate, since the majority of the passages in the Torah recount the early history of salvation for the Jews, and for Christians as well.

word for love is *ahabah*, commonly directed to other human beings, with the exception of parents. *Hesed* commonly is translated by two words, such as "covenant love," or "steadfast love," and sometimes by "mercy," since the Septuagint frequently translates it as *eleos* ("mercy"). Since mercy in the Old Testament is so frequently mentioned in association with *hesed*, or covenant love, it is worth examining.

STUDY

The sole passage where God shows mercy in the Pentateuch is Exodus 33:19.

 Stop here and read **Exodus 33:19** in your own Bible.

The context begins in Exodus 32, where Moses is still on Mount Sinai, receiving the instructions on how to build the Ark of the Covenant, the tabernacle, the altars, and the area designated for worship. The people grow impatient with his delay, so they tell his brother, Aaron, to fashion a golden calf for them to worship. By this request they break the First Commandment.

Moses has just finished receiving God's instructions and is coming down the mountain when he hears the sound of the reveling before the calf idol and then sees it. He smashes the tablets of the Ten Commandments, breaks the golden calf, burns and grounds it into dust, and scatters it over their drinking water, thereby making the people sick. With the help of his fellow Levites, he attacks those who still want to worship the calf and kills three thousand of them.

After purging the people of their sin, Moses returns to speak to the Lord on Mount Sinai saying,

"Alas, this people have sinned a great sin; they have made for themselves gods of gold. But now, if you will forgive their sin — and if not, blot me, I beg you, out of your book which you have written." (Ex 32:31-32, RSV-SCE)

The Lord responds,

"Whoever has sinned against me, him will I blot out of my book. But now go, lead the people to the place of which I have spoken to you; behold, my angel shall go before you. Nevertheless, in the day when I visit, I will visit their sin upon them." And the LORD sent a plague upon the people, because they made the calf which Aaron made." (Ex 32:33-35)

Obviously, breaking the First Commandment is an enormously big deal, and God punishes them severely, threatening not to continue leading them into the Promised Land. In this very tense situation, Moses intercedes for the people. In response to Moses' intercession, the Lord then promises, "My presence will go with you, and I will give you rest" (Ex 33:14). Still, Moses wants to make sure of the Lord's presence and intercedes a second time, saying that it is only God's presence among Israelites that makes them distinct from the rest of the people on earth.

Therefore God answers Moses, "This very thing that you have spoken I will do; for you have found favor in my sight, and I know you by name" (Ex 33:17, RSV-SCE).

Yet Moses intercedes yet a third time, "I beg you, show me your glory" (Ex 33:18, RSV-SCE), and the Lord answers with four promises: "I will make all my goodness pass before you, and will proclaim before you my name 'The LORD'; and I will be gracious to whom I will be gracious, and will show mercy [MT rahamti; Septuagint oiktireso] on whom I will show mercy [MT arahem; Septuagint oiktiro]" (Ex 33:19).

This promise is fulfilled immediately afterward when Moses returns to the mountain and the Lord passes by him to show Moses his glory. At that point the Lord says:

"The LORD, the LORD, a God merciful [MT rahum; Septuagint oiktirmon] and gracious [MT hanun; Septuagint eleemon], slow to anger, and abounding in steadfast love [hesed] and faithfulness, keeping steadfast love [hesed] for thousands, forgiving iniquity and transgression and sin, but who will by no means clear the guilty, visiting the iniquity of the fathers upon the children and the children's children, to the third and the fourth generation." (Ex 34:6-7)

CONSIDER

Think back on the episodes about Abraham, Isaac, and Jacob, each of whom sinned, particularly by lying, yet their sin was not severely chastised. Neither is there a history of sin described for the four-hundred-year period of sojourn in Egypt, which is mostly passed over in silence. Even the various times when the Israelites complained during the plagues and the departure from Egypt are not punished.

Fashioning the golden calf and worshiping it occasions the first serious chastisement of the people of Israel, and it becomes a model of Israel's sin and punishment in the future. However, this same episode is the first occasion for the Lord to speak a promise of mercy to his people. Moses makes a request for himself: he wants the Lord to show him his glory. He has spent the previous forty days on Sinai, fasting and listening to God's instructions. Upon returning to his people, he deals with the crisis of the golden calf, including the Lord's threat to abandon the people to the care of an angel. Now he seeks personal assurance of the Lord's ongoing presence, with the request to see the Lord's glory. In response, the Lord promises three things: first, Moses will see the Lord's "goodness" (not quite all of his glory); he will proclaim his name (as he had done at the burning bush); and he will be gracious and merciful.

This last promise is the concern of this present study. The most important point is that God chooses to be gracious and merciful to whomever he wants; therefore, humans cannot control him in this regard.

However, the terms he uses are significant. The Hebrew verb for "be gracious" is *hanan*, from which is derived the noun *hen*, meaning "grace," and the name John, *Yohannan*, meaning "the Lord is gracious." The word translated as "mercy" is *raham*, also frequently translated as "show compassion" or "be compassionate." The word comes from the term for "womb" (*rehem*), suggesting an image of the safe, warm, comfortable, and protective womb as the idea for compassion. The Greek translation for the verb in this verse is *oiktiro*, which denotes the expression of lament for someone or pity for him. It most typically translates either the Hebrew *hanan* (ten times) or *raham* (twelve times). Yet, note that after this, the Lord's first self-definition as being merciful, he also states that he is great in steadfast love — that is, *hesed*, the love particular to the covenant. Even though Israel is unfaithful, the Lord remains faithful to his covenantal love. This covenantal love (*hesed*) is key to this first appearance of God's mercy in the Bible, and it will continue from this point on as a regular partner of God's mercy throughout Scripture.

Perhaps the most significant point to make about the Lord's promise of being gracious and showing mercy/compassion is its connection in this passage to his promise to remain present to Israel. Certainly, the rest of the Pentateuch mentions other occasions of sin, punishment, and reconciliation, but God's continuing presence remains assured. Here alone, because of the sin against the First Commandment by making the golden calf, the very core of the covenant relationship between the Lord and Israel is at risk, and therefore God threatens to abandon the people to an angel. However, at Moses' prophetic intercession, the Lord promises to remain present to the people and at the same time promises to show grace and compassionate mercy in the future — as he personally determines.

STUDY

Covenant love and mercy show up in the prophetic texts of reconciliation, which include Hosea, Jeremiah, Isaiah, and Daniel.

Hosea

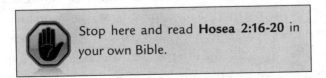

Stop here and read **Hosea 2:16-20** in your own Bible.

Hosea announces events that will happen "on that day," a phrase that referred to the day of the Lord as a day of judgment. It first appears in Exodus 32:34 "in the day when I visit, I will visit their sin upon them," which is the threat after the golden-calf narrative and before the first promise of mercy.

THE PROPHET AND THE PROSTITUTE

Hosea, a prophet in northern Israel from the 740s to the 720s, was told to become a living parable of the Lord's relationship with unfaithful Israel. He was told to marry Gomer, a "woman of prostitutions" (cf. Hos 1:2), have three children, and give them names symbolic of Israel's infidelities to the Lord.

The first step in describing this restoration of the covenant is that the people will no longer call the Lord "my Baal" but "my husband." Baal is the name of the chief god of the Canaanites, whom Israel had worshiped as the source of their "grain, the wine, and the oil" (Hos 2:22), and other products of their prosperity. The worship of Baal was considered "harlotry" and "adultery," terms used to describe the worship of other deities. However, Baal is also a term meaning "husband," though in the sense of being lord and master. In Hosea, the Lord will be called by the more acceptable term for husband, indicating that a restoration of this marital-like relationship is in fact a restoration of the covenant between Israel and the Lord.

The quality of this marriage-like covenant will be its eternity, righteousness, justice, covenant love, mercy, faithfulness, and knowledge of the Lord. Compare this with the description of the renewal of the covenant in Exodus 34:6-7, where mercy is also alongside steadfast love (hesed) and faithfulness. Consider also that the people of the northern Kingdom of Israel had worshiped golden calves at Bethel and Dan, a sin also parallel to the renewal of the covenant after the golden-calf episode. Doubtless, Hosea made this connection and wanted his contemporaries to see it, too.

Jeremiah

Stop here and read **Jeremiah 33:25-26** in your own Bible.

Jeremiah came from Anathoth, a town on the border of Judah and the Northern Kingdom. His prophetic career began around 627 B.C., almost a hundred years after the fall of Samaria, the capital of the Northern Kingdom. He may well have had a positive influence on the reign and religious reforms of King Josiah, but after the king's death in 609 B.C., Jeremiah was not heeded by Josiah's successors. He had warned the people about their many sins and against engaging the tottering superpower of Egypt against the rising superpower of Babylon, but no one listened. In 587 B.C., Jerusalem was defeated and destroyed by the Babylonians. Jeremiah did not gloat at all; like the rest of the prophets, after they were shown to have truly spoken the word of the Lord, he then spoke many prophecies of comfort and hope.

After oracles confirming that the Lord will be faithful to his unconditional covenant with David by restoring a ruler from David's direct line, Jeremiah then turns to a complaint being made by the conquering Babylonians and their allies. The Babylonians have interpreted their defeat of Judah and the destruction of the Temple in Jerusalem as a sign that the Lord has rejected Israel and Judah from being his people. Remember, the covenant had been defined by the Lord being their God and Israel being his people. The Babylonians' statement is their idea that the covenant has been irreparably broken.

The Lord responds to that analysis by comparing his covenant with Jacob and David to his covenant with the day and the night or the heavens and the earth. Since he will not reject his covenant with the forces of nature that continue their laws and regular process, neither will he break his covenant with Jacob and the family of David, who will rule over the seed of Abraham, Isaac, and Jacob, the founders of the nation. The restoration of their fortunes and the Lord's mercy is possible only because he will remain faithful to the covenant. While the term *hesed*, or "steadfast love," is not linked with mercy, the restoration of the covenant is explicitly the background that makes mercy possible. Mercy, as the forgiveness of sin and reconciliation of the people and king, is only possible because the Lord remains faithful to his covenant relationship, even after the people fail to be faithful by committing sins.

Isaiah

Isaiah 56-66 are an addition to the book that was composed after the return from the Babylonian Exile (538 B.C.), and after the rebuilding of the Temple in Jerusalem in the time of the Persian king Darius (515 B.C.). The composition may well have continued into the fifth century B.C., since Isaiah 61:2 mentions the "year of the Lord's favor," probably a reference to the Jubilee Year in 473 B.C. As the other prophets had foretold, the people of Judah returned home and restored their worship in the Temple. Yet, even after such marvelous fulfillment of prophecies, life was not at all perfect or ideal. Some sinners, particularly from the leadership and elites, still oppressed and caused problems for the rest of the people.

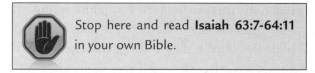

Stop here and read **Isaiah 63:7-64:11** in your own Bible.

These passages are a literary form known as "community lament" — that is, the people's prayer within a difficult situation. The preceding prophecies were proclamations of great salvation, but they contrasted with the actual situation of the community's problems in Jerusalem. However, people of faith do not deny either God's promise or their present plight but turn toward him and let both realities take shape in a prayer addressed directly to the Lord.

Isaiah 63:7-16 treats the Lord's dealing with Israel, especially during the Exodus from Egypt. The passage opens with the prophet's announcement that he will recount the Lord's love and the past worship. He describes the Lord's steadfast love (using the plural form of *hesed*), his praises and goodness as gifts he has granted to Israel in accord with his mercy and steadfast or covenant love. He recognizes that not only are his covenant love and goodness gifts freely bestowed by the Lord, but even Israel's past ability and opportunities to praise him are his gifts too. At the same time, he recognizes that these gifts are bestowed according to the measure of his mercy and covenant love, God's characteristics that once again go together.

This is a sophisticated celebration, in that even though the Lord's commitment to Israel is true covenant love, it is also completely undeserved. The people are rebellious, and they can do nothing to truly earn the Lord's love, yet his gifts are bestowed on the basis of his mercy and covenant love. Every believer can only stand back and express amazement at God's love in one's own life.

When the Lord reflects back on Israel's history, he states that he assumed he could trust them because they "are my people" (Is 63:8). They have redefined themselves in terms of the covenant with him. Their afflictions became his own, so he pitied them in their misery, particularly their slavery in Egypt.

However, the Lord's confidence was met with Israel's rebellion, a theme from the beginning of the wilderness journey and including the golden-calf episode, as well as their initial refusal to conquer Canaan. The Lord became their enemy by punishing them after the golden calf and by forcing them to wander in the desert for forty years after their first refusal to enter Canaan.

The lament continues that even though the Lord remembered "Moses his servant" and saved Israel, the prophet has to ask, "Where is he" now (Is 63:11)? Moses brought the people out of the Red Sea, and the Spirit of the Lord gave them rest, but where is the Lord now?

The prophet then raises a petitionary prayer for the Lord to look down upon the post-exilic people to see their difficulties, as he had seen the afflictions of Israel in Egypt. The prayer implies a lament when it asks about the past: "Where are your zeal and your might?" (Is 63:15). The reason for this question is that the Lord is presently withholding his compassion (plural form *rahamim*, which is usually translated as "mercy") and empathetic yearning for Israel.

The prayer continues with two reasons that the Lord should answer the petition. First, the Lord is a Father and therefore a Redeemer; hence, he should revive that paternal love and redeem Jerusalem. Second, the people's ancestors — Abraham and his grandson Israel — do not acknowledge their descendants; therefore, they have only the Lord to care for them.

Daniel

Israel's first experience of receiving God's mercy came after their communal sin of worshiping the golden calf, thereby breaking the First Commandment. The prophets generally directed the whole nation to a need for mercy in light of the whole nation's sins. In light of the whole nation's need for mercy, communal repentance is found in a number of psalms and in other passages, including the Book of Daniel.

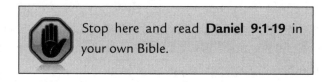

Stop here and read **Daniel 9:1-19** in your own Bible.

This text begins with historical notes that date it to the first year of the Persian king Darius (522-521 B.C.). This chapter refers to Jeremiah's prophecy of seventy years of Jerusalem's "desolations." Daniel understands the fulfillment of Jeremiah's prophecies as an occasion for prayer, fasting, penance, and a community confession of sins.

The actual prayer opens with a profession of faith in the Lord. He is both "great and terrible" ("fearful" in Hebrew), and yet he keeps the covenant and its "steadfast love" (Hebrew *hesed*; Greek *eleos*, or "mercy"). Since the covenant includes stipulations — namely, the commandments — this love is not based on emotion but on the commitment to maintain the covenant's relationship and the stipulations that support it. The Lord also looks for people to "love" him.

The rest of this prayer sets human beings in stark contrast with the Lord by the communal confession that "we have sinned."

A short confession of faith in the Lord as the one who possesses righteousness is followed by a much longer confession of confusion among the whole people of Israel, whether at home or in exile, because of their sinful "treachery" against the Lord.

Another confession of faith in the Lord contrasts the sinful people with him. A statement of faith announces that the Lord possesses mercy and forgiveness. The Hebrew for "mercy" is *rahamim*, the plural form of "compassion," but the Septuagint uses *dikaiosune*, meaning "righteousness." However, the Hebrew for "forgiveness" (*selohoth*, like *rahamim*, is a plural noun) is translated in Greek as *eleos*, usually translated as "mercy." The Hebrew makes clear that "mercy" is parallel to forgiveness. Though the Greek translator was somewhat loose in his choice of vocabulary, he still sees "mercy" as the gift of God's forgiveness to his sinful people.

Next Daniel explains the reason that the Lord needs to show mercy and forgiveness: the people "rebelled" (*maradnu*) against him — a most serious term for sin — by disobeying his laws. Daniel recognizes that the people deserve the curses threatened through Moses in Deuteronomy 26-27, but the Lord's mercy and forgiveness are the way out of the curses.

Daniel then speaks directly to his fellow sinners about the Lord's just punishment, to convince them that the Lord has acted rightly toward them through the calamities they experienced, such as the destruction of Jerusalem.

Daniel explains that the whole calamity came upon the nation fully in accord with the threats made in the "law of Moses," again, a reference to the curses of Deuteronomy 26-27. He adds a new level of blame by convicting the people of not having sought out the Lord's favor and grace in prayer, with a repentance that turns away from iniquities in order to turn to the Lord's truth. He states the stark reality that "the LORD our God is righteous" in all that he does (Dan 9:14); by refusing to obey him, we humans have moved into the realm of sin and iniquity.

Daniel then returns to addressing the Lord directly, identifying him as "our God," because his previous address to the people brought them to the point of accepting their responsibility for having sinned and received the threatened punishments.

Daniel identifies "[the] LORD our God" as the one "who brought your people out of the land of Egypt" (Dan 9:15, RSV-SCE) and recognizing the restoration of the covenant in two ways. First, the opening line of the statement of covenantal stipulations — that is, the Ten Commandments — states, "I am the LORD your God, who brought you out of the land of Egypt, out of the house of bondage" (Ex 20:2). As was typical of ancient covenants, the name and title of the one making the covenant is given. Second, Exodus 20:2 is a statement of the history of the Lord's past deeds toward his covenant partner. Even as Daniel reestablishes the fact that Israel still belongs to the covenant, he makes another confession of national sin and wickedness.

The prayer continues with a petition asking the Lord to be motivated by "all your righteous acts" (Dan 9:16, RSV-SCE). The Lord's righteousness is the basis for asking the Lord to turn away his anger and wrath from Jerusalem. Another motive for forgiving the nation's sins is that the surrounding peoples have made Israel a byword, the subject of international gossip and criticism. The Lord's forgiveness will bring such negative talk to an end.

Daniel adds another motive for the Lord to answer their prayer: to do so for the Lord's own sake, since it is his sanctuary, the Temple, the place where he is worshiped, that will be restored if the Lord forgives the people.

Finally, Daniel asks "my God" (Dan 9:18) to hear the petition. This appeal on the basis of his special relationship with God is another reason for the Lord to help Jerusalem, his city.

Ultimately, the Lord will not answer Daniel's petitions to protect Jerusalem because the people deserve it as morally righteous folk. Repeatedly, he has admitted that they are sinners and not righteous. Rather, the Lord's "great mercy" is the basis for answering them in their situation of great need. Here the Hebrew term is the plural form of "compassion," which both the Greek and English translate as the singular word "mercy."

Daniel is confident that the Lord still has the same compassion for Israel in his day as he had when the Lord first renewed the covenant after the golden-calf episode. Though Israel had been yet again unfaithful to the covenant, the Lord remains faithful and compassionate.

STUDY

In the Book of Sirach, attributed to the early second-century-B.C. wisdom writer, God shows humans mercy because he created them and made a covenant with them.

 Stop here and read **Sirach 16:24-18:14** in your own Bible.

This long section of Sirach treats the relationship of God's Wisdom and his mercy in four poems. The first (Sir 16:24-30) lays out the principle that God's word is the cause of the orderliness and goodness of creation. The second (Sir 17:1-24) addresses the creation of human beings, who have power over much of creation and are made in the image of God, and yet are limited by death. They have wisdom and understanding, and yet must fear the Lord, who knows all their ways and will judge them. A particularly significant section of this poem (Sir 17:11-14) mentions the covenant and its precepts:

> He bestowed knowledge upon them,
>> and allotted to them the law of life.
> He established with them an eternal covenant,
>> and showed them his judgments.
> Their eyes saw his glorious majesty,
>> and their ears heard the glory of his voice.
> And he said to them, "Beware of all unrighteousness."
>> And he gave commandment to each of them concerning his neighbor.

The eternal covenant is the source of the "law of life," which includes the precepts, judgments, and commandments he spoke to them so as to avoid unrighteousness. These verses are the link between the covenant and the offer of mercy in Sirach 17:29 and 18:11-14.

The third poem (Sir 17:25-32) turns to exhortations based on this wisdom about human abilities and responsibilities to the Lord based on their creation and the covenant. In order to live out the purpose of human life, people need to turn to the Lord and away from all types of sins — which is the very essence of repentance. Sirach backs up the exhortation with some rhetorical questions, whose answer is that people who die end up in Hades (*Sheol* in Hebrew), which was an unhappy state of the souls of the dead. (Recall that at this point in history, Israelites did not have any idea that their souls might go to heaven and enjoy eternity with God; that would come with the preaching, death, and resurrection of Jesus Christ.) Since no one can praise God in Hades, Sirach wants readers to conclude that they should live a moral life before God so that they might live longer on earth, where they are able to praise him.

From rhetorical questions, Sirach moves to clear assertions. The first is that the mercy and forgiveness of the Lord is great, therefore one's repentance from sin should be filled with hope of mercy and forgiveness. Then he reminds the reader of the weakness inherent in mortal human beings. If the light of the powerful sun can fail, so will human strength. Humbly recognize human limits, fear God, and repent by turning toward him for mercy and forgiveness.

The final poem (Sir 18:1-14) contrasts the mortal humans of the preceding poem with the eternal and infinite God who made all things in the universe. Again Sirach uses rhetorical questions to force listeners to think about God's infinite greatness and their own smallness. He asserts that no one has the power to proclaim all of God's deeds, and he challenges anyone to try to search and measure God's deeds in creation. However, these questions assume that as soon as someone claims to know all that God has done, a sage like Sirach can mention one more great deed to show that the fool who proposes an answer will be refuted on the spot.

Sirach poses questions about the nature, usefulness, virtues, and vices in human beings. After having pointed out the limits of human knowledge, he brings up here the shortness of human life to present limitations of human power. Even if a person lives to one hundred, that is extremely short in comparison to human history, yet alone in comparison to eternity — the unlimited extent of time forward and back.

Though he insists on humans being tiny like grains of sand, short lived, and sinful, Sirach still asserts that the Lord is patient with them and shows them mercy (Sir 18:11-14). If God does not show them mercy, they will end up even more evil than if he were not compassionate to them. Even his rebukes and correction, which may seem painful at the time, are meant to turn them from a dangerous path that leads to total destruction. While the Lord will certainly judge the arrogant harshly, his compassion — or, to translate consistently, "mercy" — is toward those who humbly choose to accept his discipline and judgment.

DISCUSS

1. What are some insights into the relationship between covenant love and mercy that you have discovered in this section?
2. This chapter discusses the relationship of sin, forgiveness, love, and mercy. How does God use our sinfulness to extend

forgiveness, love, and mercy? How is this shown in the relationship between God and Israel?

3. What are some aspects and qualities of covenant love? Have you experienced these in your own relationship with God?

PRACTICE

This week, consider the five types of sin listed on page 85. Examine your own life in light of these different types of offense against God. In which areas are you most in need of his mercy?

Session 5

LORD, HAVE MERCY

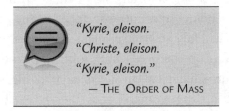

The themes of mercy and forgiveness that have their roots in the Old Testament come to full fruition in the life and person of Jesus in the New Testament. Little wonder that Jesus himself is referred to as "Divine Mercy," since it is in him that the fullness of God's mercy is revealed to the world.

The idea of mercy and covenant love fulfilled in Jesus begins in the Gospel of Luke. In it, "mercy" is mentioned ten times, with five instances in chapter 1: in the Blessed Virgin Mary's Magnificat, during the Visitation to Elizabeth, and at the birth of John the Baptist.

ARAMAIC AND GREEK

Luke 1-2, though written in Greek, is a translation from a document that had been composed in Aramaic, as evidenced by grammatical structures that are odd, if not barbaric, in the Greek but translate well into standard Semitic forms of speech. This is relevant because the uses of "mercy" in Luke 1 are quite at home in a Semitic, Old Testament background, which lies behind their usage here.

STUDY

 Stop here and read **Luke 1:39-55** in your own Bible.

Because of the angel Gabriel's news that Elizabeth is also with child, Mary takes her own initiative to travel to the Judean hill country to visit her. The Holy Spirit becomes very active within Elizabeth and the infant John inside her womb: John leaps like a lamb within her womb, while Elizabeth pronounces two blessings on Mary, "Blessed are you among women" and "Blessed is she who believed that there would be a fulfillment of what was spoken to her from the Lord," plus a beatitude on the infant Jesus, "the fruit" of Mary's womb.

The Blessed Virgin Mary, also filled with the Holy Spirit, responds with a hymn of joy and praise to God for all that he has done with her personally and with the nation as a whole. She expresses her personal experience of "magnifying" and "rejoicing" in God as Savior and sets forth the reasons for her joy as the Lord's consideration of her lowliness and the "great things" he has done for her. All generations will proclaim the Virgin Mary as "blessed," just as Elizabeth has already announced, in this act of salvation that God has accomplished in the incarnation of his Son in her womb; he is holy.

She then turns her attention toward the history of salvation in all of Israel in every generation, as a way to see the incarnation of God the Son in her womb as the fulfillment of the whole of sacred history. The history of Israel, going back to Abraham and his "seed," is presented here as a history of mercy from beginning to end. Mary goes on to say that "his mercy [*eleos*] is on those who fear him from generation to generation."

INVESTIGATE

"FEAR OF THE LORD" AND MERCY (NO. 1)

 Look up the following passages and make notes on the relation between "fear of the Lord" and mercy.

PASSAGE	NOTES
Nehemiah 1:11	
Tobit 14:6-7	
Judith 16:15	
Psalm 103:8-17	
Psalm 119:73-75	

Sirach 2:7-18	
Jeremiah 42:11-17	
Habakkuk 3:2	

The nature of God's mercy is further explained by the ways that the Lord scatters proud, arrogant people, removes the mighty from thrones and power, and sends the rich away empty: such is his action toward those who do not fear him. However, the lowly, the poor, and the hungry who do fear him will experience exaltation and good things.

Mary continues by explaining that this child growing in her womb fulfills the promises of the unconditional covenants and personifies God's mercy.

CONSIDER

The next references to mercy in Luke occur in the passages about the birth of the Baptist.

 Stop here and read Luke **1:57-79** in your own Bible.

The birth of Elizabeth's son and the joyful response of her neighbors and relatives set the scene for the dramatic events and words at the celebration of the circumcision of John the Baptist. St. Luke mentions the eighth day, when the boy was to be circumcised, the sign of becoming a member of the people of Israel by entering into the covenant God had made with Abraham. Although it was expected that the boy would be named after his father, his mother said he would be called "John."

The neighbors and relatives turn from Elizabeth to Zechariah, who was still mute after having asked the angel Gabriel, "How shall I know this?" (Lk 1:18). Zechariah's question to the angel was a request for proof, while the angel was seeking faith. Therefore the proof would be his muteness until the child was born. Clearly Zechariah learned his lesson and remained obedient to the Lord by naming his son "John" (which means "the Lord is gracious"), just as the angel had commanded him. At that point, Zechariah could speak, starting off with praise of God as his first words.

The content of Zechariah's praise of God is his great hymn, now commonly known by its Latin name, the Benedictus. St. Luke adds his own editorial note that Zechariah was filled with the Holy Spirit and was prophesying in this hymn. This demonstrates Zechariah's renewed faith in what God can do, speaking words of praise and blessing to God as the Holy Spirit directed him.

The majority of his hymn is directed to praising God for visiting and redeeming his people by raising up the "horn of salvation" (Lk 1:69) in the house of David. Since Zechariah and his son, John, are Levites, he is referring here to the infant Jesus, still in the womb of the Virgin Mary. Mary has spent three months with Zechariah and Elizabeth, who learned from her of the virginal conception and the promise from the same angel Gabriel that Mary's child would inherit the throne of his father, David. Zechariah's faith has so expanded that he recognizes that even though his son is born miraculously, the conception of Jesus in the Virgin's womb is a miracle far beyond the birth of John. Zechariah's Holy Spirit-inspired words recognize that John's role is subordinate to Jesus, and Zechariah readily accepts that fact in this hymn of praise.

Zechariah's hymn begins with the recognition that the Lord has fulfilled the covenant and the promises made through the ancestors. Note the words "remember his holy covenant" (Lk 1:72). The name Zechariah means "the Lord remembered." This pun only works in the Aramaic original lying behind the whole of the Infancy Narratives, just as the pun on Elizabeth's name (*Elishaba* in Hebrew and Aramaic, meaning "God will satisfy") appears in the Semitic text of the Magnificat.

The promise of mercy is mentioned here in the context of the covenant that the Lord has remembered. This, as noted in the Old Testament passages, is a typical connection between mercy and the covenant. In this context, as in the Magnificat, the unconditional covenant with Abraham is in mind. Therefore mercy is not about reconciliation after sins are committed but rather about deliverance from the enemies who hate God's people.

Only in the second part does Zechariah address his son, John. While Jesus is a horn of salvation, Zechariah's son, John, is a "prophet of the Most High" (Lk 1:76). His task will be to precede Jesus and prepare his ways by giving people knowledge of salvation through forgiveness of sins. This section emphasizes that the "tender mercy of our God" is Christ, the rising dawn, who will give light to those sitting "in darkness and in the shadow of death" (Lk 1:78-79). Again, mercy is not about forgiveness and reconciliation but more about the deliverance of people in grave danger — namely, the darkness of this world.

STUDY

As we move on in Jesus' ministry, two major themes of mercy appear in the New Testament, both of which have roots in the Old Testament. The first is that mercy relieves people from afflictions, such as demonic influence and endangerment, and from various illnesses. Mercy is used in regard to freedom from a demonic spirit and from blindness (in the Book of Tobit), which may have influenced the New Testament use of the term in regard to these issues. The second issue in the New Testament is the necessity of showing mercy to other people in order to receive it from the Lord God. This, too, is rooted in the Old Testament background.

Seeking Mercy from Demons, Disease, and Disasters

A number of passages from the Old and New Testaments explicitly connect the request for mercy with situations in which people are afflicted by demons or disease (leprosy, specifically). These passages occur within various prayers in the Psalms and within narratives describing events where mercy is extended to people suffering from these afflictions. It is important to see that mercy belongs not only to the realm of forgiveness for sins but also for easing very difficult and even deadly afflictions.

One psalm that addresses these concerns is familiar to many: Psalm 23.

 Stop here and read **Psalm 23** in your own Bible.

The first three verses are a confession of faith in the Lord, which describes him in the third person as the good shepherd who leads

THE VALLEY OF THE SHADOW OF DEATH

This valley is a deep ravine known as Wadi Qelt, running just west of Jerusalem. The old Roman road between Jericho and Jerusalem runs along its ridge, as it rises from the 1,200 feet below sea level, where Jericho lies, to the 2,500 feet above sea level of the Mount of Olives. Shepherds still lead their sheep along its high cliffs to bring them from the winter pastures of the warmer Jordan Valley to the summer pastures of the cooler highlands, where they can graze the grain fields after the harvest and re-fertilize them to the farmers' benefit. However, the journey is quite difficult, even for sure-footed sheep and donkeys.

the psalmist, who compares himself to a sheep. However, the images of shepherding turn to the distinctively human concerns in verse 3: the Lord restores my soul and leads me in paths of righteousness for the sake of his name.

The center of this psalm (verses 4 and 5) is a prayer in direct address, speaking now to the Lord as "you." The psalmist knows that life has dangers, such as walking through "the valley of the shadow of death."

For humans, "the valley of the shadow of death" is an image for the tremendous difficulties and risks of life. The psalmist recognizes that the only reason not to fear evil and danger is that the Lord is present with him, and his shepherd's staff will protect him. Ultimately, after the journey, the psalmist speaks to the Lord about his assurance that the Lord has prepared a banquet, with an anointing of oil and overflowing wine. This hope keeps him going forward, the way that the sheep move through the Valley of the Shadow of Death, with the hope of refreshing pastures ahead of them.

The psalm concludes with another confession of faith in the benefits hoped for. Goodness and mercy are the first benefits. "Mercy" translates the Hebrew *hesed*, both in English and in the Septuagint. The Hebrew nuance of the word refers to the covenantal love that God has for Israel, and vice versa, as we discussed earlier. This is the committed love that chooses the other person in all circumstances. The other great benefit is dwelling in the Lord's house forever, a reference to the Temple in Jerusalem, which would be the goal of the journey from Jericho, if one went through the Valley of the Shadow of Death. The psalmist will be able to pray and worship there forever.

Of course, Christians have read a number of their own aspects into this psalm of faith and trust. The hope for a banquet and overflowing cup has been compared to the Eucharist, and the anointing to the chrism placed upon believers at Baptism and Confirmation. Further, the hope of dwelling in the house of the Lord forever is seen as an image of heaven.

INVESTIGATE

THE BOOK OF TOBIT

 While we cannot go into great detail here, the Book of Tobit is one Old Testament source for our background on healing and deliverance from demons. The Book of Tobit was probably written in the third century B.C., though some place it earlier. The Greek manuscripts were the earliest copies available, but among the Dead Sea scrolls found in Cave IV were a Hebrew and two Aramaic copies of Tobit, so scholars are not sure in which of those two languages it was written.

It is suggested that you read the story of Tobit yourself before continuing with our look at the New Testament texts. Note particularly the afflictions that are suffered and the use of the word "mercy" throughout the text.

Basically, the book concerns an Israelite, Tobit, living in Nineveh after the Assyrian destruction of his homeland. He remained a pious Israelite who acted righteously even at the risk of his life and safety. However, after such one good deed he took a nap, during which bird droppings fell into both eyes, blinding him. His misery increased until he prayed for death.

At the same time, a young woman named Sarah, who had been widowed seven times on seven different wedding nights, also prayed for death.

The book progresses as Tobit decides to send his only child, Tobias, to collect a debt from Raguel, the father of the above-mentioned Sarah. God sends the angel Raphael, in human form, to guide Tobias, and they set out on their journey. Upon arrival in Ecbatana, Raphael instructs Tobias on God's plan for him to marry Sarah, but Tobias objects out of fear of the demon that killed her other husbands. Raphael responds with instructions on how to drive away the evil spirit. Raphael assures Tobias that God will answer because he is merciful and will save them and have mercy. Furthermore, their marriage is God's will for them and their children. Both the promise of mercy and the understanding of God's purpose open Tobias' heart to falling deeply in love with Sarah.

Clearly, mercy is God's gift, but it is not oriented toward the forgiveness of sin but toward deliverance from a demon. This understanding of mercy will be very important in the Gospels too. Tobit 6:17 is the first passage that explicitly links mercy with freedom from the demonic, and it offers an insight into the mentality of the people who petitioned Jesus for an exorcism as an act of mercy.

STUDY

Given the Old Testament understanding of mercy, we will now examine some New Testament passages where people approach Jesus with problems such as leprosy, blindness, and demon possession. All of them will petition him, "Have mercy [*eleison*] on me," very much in continuity with the psalms of lament and with Tobit.

Leprosy at the time of Jesus was what we now call Hansen's disease, a bacterial infection that can affect not only the respiratory tract, nerves, and eyes but also cause skin lesions and ulcers that can greatly disfigure the victims. The disease had been introduced to the region three hundred years earlier by soldiers of Alexander the Great, after their return from a campaign in India. With no cure even remotely possible, its victims were considered "walking corpses," both because of their inevitable doom and of the body's process of decay even during life. The ancients did not understand how it spread, so lepers were to be completely quarantined, with no direct contact with the healthy.

 Stop here and read **Luke 17:12-19** in your own Bible.

Since lepers could associate together, ten of them see Jesus from a distance as he enters a village. They have to shout their petition to Jesus, whom they address as "Master." "Have mercy [*eleison*] on us" is their plea, not in the sense of forgiving their sins but in order to pity them and help them.

Jesus responds with a command to show themselves to the priests, which was the beginning of the process of re-admittance into the community. Leviticus 13 lays out the detailed regulations by which the priests were to determine whether a person had leprosy (which did not refer to Hansen's disease at the time of Moses but to other skin disorders), followed by Leviticus 14, which details the sacrifices and ceremonies celebrating the cleansing of a leper. This would have been both an act of faith in Jesus' word and an act of obedience to the Law of Moses.

The cleansing of these lepers takes place as they go on their way, but one of them, a Samaritan, returns to Jesus, praising God and thanking Jesus. Samaritans were a mix of Israelites and some pagan settlers in central Israel after the destruction of the Northern Kingdom. They had established their own temple on Mount Gerizim rather than worship in Jerusalem; they had their own version of the Torah; and they antagonized the Judeans, who returned the favor. However, the Samaritan is the only leper to offer praise to God and thanks to Jesus.

Jesus then addresses the people around him with three rhetorical questions that both inform them of the cleansing of the lepers and the appropriateness of praising God when mercy is extended. Then he addresses the healed Samaritan with a word of assurance, again parallel to the statements of confidence in Tobit, informing him that his faith has made him well. This faith is demonstrated not by a profession of some creedal statement but by praise and thanksgiving.

CONSIDER

Those whom Jesus heals often began by crying out, "Have mercy on us."

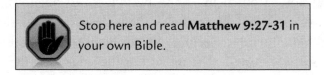

Stop here and read **Matthew 9:27-31** in your own Bible.

This episode begins with two blind men initiating the miracle by crying out to Jesus as he passes by, "Have mercy on us" — again in the sense of healing a situation that neither they nor any human physician of the day could heal. They call him "Son of David," which is their recognition that he is the Messiah, who would descend from David's line.

The next stage of the miracle is a closer, more personal encounter wherein Jesus questions them directly about their faith in his ability to do this miracle. He does not demand faith in his divinity at this point but in the ability to heal as only God is capable. In response to and in the measure of their faith, Jesus heals them, and they are able to see. While they have great faith in him, they are not so good at obeying his order to be quiet about the miracle. Jesus regularly commands people not to speak about a healing or exorcism because he does not want faith to be based on the miracles; rather, he wants miracles to be based on faith.

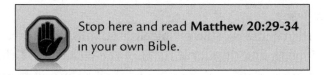

Stop here and read **Matthew 20:29-34** in your own Bible.

Parallel to this healing of the blind in Galilee, two more blind men in Jericho, just a few miles to the east of Jerusalem, cry out, "Have mercy on us, Son of David." This time, near Passover in a busy city, a crowd interacts with the blind men, ordering them to be silent. However, these blind men refuse to obey the crowd, and they shout out their plea for mercy all the more loudly and insistently.

As in the first healing of the blind, Jesus meets with the two men more intimately, asking them to specify their request for mercy. They want their eyes opened, showing that mercy here refers to an act of salvation from being blind bystanders to openly following the path of God that Jesus shows them. Jesus touches their eyes "in pity," more literally, "feeling pity" in his internal organs (Greek *splagchnistheis*, feeling a stirring within the *splagchna*, the term for internal organs). The scene of Jesus speaking so personally to the two men evokes this deep-seated compassion or pity. That feeling of compassion motivates Jesus to open their eyes. They, presumably in gratitude, immediately follow Jesus on his way to Jerusalem, where they will witness the greatest of his miracles: his death on the cross that leads to his glorious resurrection.

STUDY

Several Gospel episodes relate pleas for mercy, which Jesus answers by exorcizing demons. We can read these in light of Raguel's prayer, where mercy refers to the deliverance of Tobias and Sarah from the demon Asmodeus (Tobit 8:9-17).

The Canaanite Woman

 Stop here and read **Matthew 15:21-28** in your own Bible.

Jesus goes into the district of Tyre and Sidon after an intense dispute with the Pharisees. Since the Pharisees and Herodians are collaborating to trap Jesus — and perhaps have him executed by Herod, as John the Baptist had been — Jesus enters the Syrophoenician territory because it is outside the dominion and influence of Herod, who wants to kill him.

A Canaanite woman approaches Jesus with the cry, "Have mercy on me." The nature of this mercy is explained by her daughter's severe possession by a demon. Mercy again refers to a saving act that is a help to the woman and her daughter. Interestingly, this gentile woman identifies Jesus as "Lord" and "Son of David." David had been an ally of Hiram, the king of Tyre, as had his son Solomon. Now she recognizes the lordship of the Messianic descendant of David in her plea for mercy, to free her daughter from demonic possession.

The rest of the interaction between Jesus and this woman takes the form of a wisdom debate common in the Middle East. The disciples understand her only as a distraction to be dismissed, but Jesus raises the issue of his mission being primarily directed to Israel. When she continues to plea for help, Jesus contrasts the bread he was sent to give to the children of Israel and the unfairness of giving it to the dogs. She trumps this wisdom by saying that even the dogs get the crumbs that fall off the table. Jesus recognizes her use of proverbial wisdom in her persistent petition for mercy and help as a sign of the faith — a "great faith" — he also sought from the other people who came to him for mercy. As a result, her daughter is healed.

The Epileptic Boy

Stop here and read **Matthew 17:14-18** in your own Bible.

Jesus, Peter, James, and John are just coming down from the Transfiguration when they encounter an agitated crowd. One man in the crowd approaches Jesus, asking for mercy on his epileptic son who suffers often by falling into water and fire. This request for mercy concerns a hope that Jesus can save the boy from such suffering.

Unlike the other episodes where people expressed great faith when they sought mercy, the disciples and the crowd are critiqued by Jesus as "faithless," which is a key to their being perverse too. Nonetheless, Jesus rebukes the spirit, and the boy is cured instantly in spite of their lack of faith. He shows mercy here as yet another act of salvation that saves someone's life.

In Mark's version, the dialogue with the father is more detailed, indicating that at first the father of the boy has a conditional kind of faith in Jesus.

Stop here and read **Mark 9:14-29** in your own Bible.

Jesus rebukes him and exhorts him to accept the doctrine that everything is possible for the person who believes. The father gives a classic answer that reflects the faith of so many people: "I believe;

help my unbelief!" (Mk 9:24). He knows that his faith is lacking, but he trusts that Jesus can even help him move toward a deeper level of faith. Faith requires the grace of God, for which reason the Church identifies it as a "theological virtue," along with hope and love.

The Gerasene Demoniac

 Stop here and read **Mark 5:1-20** in your own Bible.

Jesus crossed the Sea of Galilee, to its eastern shore, to the area of Gerasa, where gentile populations dominated.

GERASA

 Gerasa (modern Jerash) was a flourishing Greco-Roman city whose ruins are still very impressive. In Matthew 8:28 — which describes the same incident, although now there are two men — the demoniacs are said to be among "the Gadarenes."

Upon his arrival, Jesus is met by a man possessed by demons, who lived among the tombs, naked, wild, and uncontrollable. The power of God confronts this demon-possessed man, who says:

> "What have you to do with me, Jesus, Son of the Most High God? I adjure you by God, do not torment me." For he had said to him, "Come out of the man, you unclean spirit!" And Jesus asked him, 'What is your name?' He replied, 'My name is Legion; for we are many." (Mk 5:7-9)

The demons beg Jesus to let them stay in the region rather than return to hell. However, as is typical of the self-destructive forces of evil, the demons drive the two thousand swine into the sea, where they drown, even though pigs are good swimmers. The swineherds flee to tell the townspeople, who come out to see what has happened. Seeing the demoniac "clothed and in his right mind" (Mk 5:15), they beg Jesus to leave their region. Apparently, it was more difficult for them to deal with Jesus' superior power to deliver from demons than it was to accept the naked, wild demoniac's presence among them.

As Jesus is embarking to leave, the delivered demoniac begs once again, but this time it is to remain with Jesus. However, Jesus refuses, telling him, "Go home to your friends, and tell them how much the Lord has done for you, and how he has had mercy [*eleison*] on you" (Mk 5:19).

CONSIDER

Mark 5:19 is the one passage where Jesus himself describes his act of deliverance from a demon as the Lord's "mercy." Elsewhere "mercy" is mentioned by the people seeking relief from leprosy, blindness, or demons.

St. Paul uses mercy in a manner similar to the preceding passages, though only once. When his fellow evangelist, Epaphroditus, took ill, the Philippian community was very concerned, since he had come from their city. However, God had mercy on him and saved him from an illness that brought him close to death. This was also a mercy to Paul, who depended on Epaphroditus and loved him as a dear brother. In this way, mercy as a saving act of healing has an impact on both the individual healed as well as on the community — St. Paul and the Philippian church.

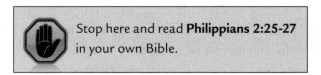
Stop here and read **Philippians 2:25-27** in your own Bible.

Though Epaphroditus was the primary recipient of the act of mercy, the whole community, near at hand and far away, shared in the joy of the act of salvation. Similarly in the laments in the Psalms, the psalmist was the main recipient of the Lord's saving mercies, but the whole community benefited. Some learned to have more faith in the Lord because of witnessing the salvation of the afflicted person; others, from the choirmaster and choir to the rest of the congregation, rejoiced in praising God for the salvation.

DISCUSS

1. Why did those who wanted healing from Jesus ask first for his mercy? How does this change your way of praying?
2. Think of the people who were angry at Jesus for having driven out a demon and causing a herd of pigs to be killed. Have you ever found yourself feeling like someone didn't deserve God's mercy? What about a murderer who repents at the last minute?
3. At Mass we pray "*Kyrie, eleison*" ("Lord, have mercy"). Knowing the context in which the lepers and the sick said this prayer, how does it change the way you might pray it the next time you attend Mass?

PRACTICE

This week, say the following Jesus Prayer, and trust in God's great mercy:

> Jesus, son of David, have mercy on me.
> Jesus, son of God, have mercy on me.
> Lord, have mercy.
> God, have mercy.

Session 6

MERCY AS A SAVING ACT

> "Jesus' attitude is striking: we do not hear words of scorn, we do not hear words of condemnation, but only words of love, of mercy, which are an invitation to conversion. 'Neither do I condemn you; go, and do not sin again" (Jn 8:11). Ah! Brothers and Sisters, God's face is the face of a merciful father who is always patient. Have you thought about God's patience, the patience he has with each one of us? That is his mercy. He always has patience, patience with us, he understands us, he waits for us, he does not tire of forgiving us if we are able to return to him with a contrite heart. 'Great is God's mercy,' says the Psalm."
>
> — POPE FRANCIS, Angelus address (March 17, 2013)

Everyone who comes to accept that he or she is a sinner makes a fundamental choice: either to despair of any escape from the punishment that sin deserves, in accord with justice, or to accept that God is merciful as well as just, and then receive mercy from him. In the early centuries of Biblical history, little is said about how to obtain mercy; proclaiming God as merciful is simply a core act of Israelite faith. The situation is roughly analogous to young children who assume that Dad and Mom always have unlimited amounts of money to spend. All one needs to do is ask, whine, perhaps pout, promise to be good — or, in final desperation, throw a tantrum.

By the time their children reach late adolescence, wise, non-indulgent parents have gradually taught them that the amount of money available is not infinite, and that in order to make money, one must work either hard, smart, or both. Similarly, in both the later Old Testament texts and in New Testament passages that build on them, people are taught that in order to receive mercy, they must show mercy to others.

STUDY

We return briefly to the Old Testament to see an example of receiving mercy after showing mercy.

 Stop here and read **Daniel 4:19-37** in your own Bible.

After having interpreted Nebuchadnezzar's dream of the statue (Dan 2), Daniel (going by his Babylonian name, Belteshazzar) interprets another dream for Nebuchadnezzar. What follows is its interpretation as "a decree of the Most High, which has come upon my lord the king" (Dan 4:24), its fulfillment in Nebuchadnezzar's life, and finally Nebuchadnezzar's praise of God as the "King of heaven," whose "works are right and his ways are just; and those who walk in pride he is able to abase" (Dan 4:37).

In verse 27, Daniel advises the king regarding how he ought to respond to the Lord's decree:

> "Therefore, O king, let my counsel be acceptable to you; break off your sins by practicing righteousness, and your iniquities by showing mercy [Hebrew *mihan*] to the oppressed, that there may perhaps be a lengthening of your tranquility."

Daniel begins with an appeal to Nebuchadnezzar's free will: "Let my counsel be acceptable to you." The king can choose whether to heed the advice or not. With the clear recognition of a real choice, Daniel offers two remedies. First, Nebuchadnezzar can break off sin by practicing righteousness, a standard term used for moral correctness in line with the standards that God has set for humanity. Second, he can turn away from his iniquities by showing mercy to the poor, oppressed people. The term "show mercy" is an infinitive form of the Aramaic verb *hanan*, a cognate to the Hebrew word for "being gracious." When Daniel calls this great king to break off sin by choosing personal righteousness, he is calling the king to an authentic life of repentance as "turning around": turn away from evil and go in the other direction toward righteousness. The other remedy is for this great and very proud king to show mercy as a form of graciousness to the "oppressed" and poor — the term means both realities. Poverty always makes people vulnerable to oppression, so they are at the mercy of the rich and powerful.

Finally, Daniel offers Nebuchadnezzar a hope that "perhaps" his tranquility may be lengthened. While this is not exactly a promise of mercy by the use of that term, it is a promise of mercy in regard to the punishment that God had decreed. Nebuchadnezzar's dream warned him of a bout of madness that would bring him down to the level of irrational animals. The promise of tranquility is the form of mercy that someone under that sentence would appropriately desire.

CONSIDER

Another Old Testament example of giving mercy in order to receive it is in Sirach. He connects fear of the Lord with the ability to receive mercy.

INVESTIGATE

"FEAR OF THE LORD" AND MERCY (NO. 2)

 Look up the following passages and make notes on "fear of the Lord" and mercy.

PASSAGE	NOTES
Sirach 1:12	

Sirach 1:18	
Sirach 1:14	
Psalm 111:10	
Proverb 1:7	

Of course, a person may have to wait for the mercy of God to show itself in his life. The Lord's timing for a merciful act may not be the same as that of the person who is suffering. However, Sirach urges a person to think carefully about the history of salvation for the whole people: everyone who trusted in the Lord was honored (not put to shame) and answered because it is the Lord's nature to be compassionate and merciful.

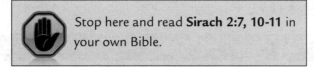

Stop here and read **Sirach 2:7, 10-11** in your own Bible.

In light of the Lord's compassion and mercy that the previous verses explain, we can look at another issue: if a person prays for the Lord to forgive his own sins, then he'd better give up his own wrath toward his enemies and forgive them. The person who shows no mercy to others will be incapable of receiving it from the Lord. As Sirach 28:4-6 says,

> Does he have no mercy [*eleos*] toward a man like himself,
>   and yet pray for his own sins?
> If he himself, being flesh, maintains wrath,
>   who will make expiation for his sins?
> Remember the end of your life, and cease from enmity,
>   remember destruction and death, and be true to the commandments.

The positive side of this principle can be found in Sirach 29:1, where showing mercy to a neighbor in need opens the way for the Lord to "strengthen" the generous person and help him keep the commandments by his grace:

> He that shows mercy [*eleos*] will lend to his neighbor,
>   and he that strengthens him with his hand keeps the commandments.

STUDY

Jesus our Lord teaches the same principles to the crowds listening to his sermons. First, humans are to be as merciful as the heavenly Father. God himself, not other humans, is the norm for the amount and kind of mercy we are to show people.

INVESTIGATE

 Look up the following passages and make notes on the giving and receiving of mercy.

PASSAGE	NOTES
Luke 6:36	
Sirach 28:4-6	
Matthew 5:7	

 Stop here and read **Mathew 23:13-36** in your own Bible.

Just as Jesus had begun his public teaching with the Beatitudes (Mt 5:3-12), so does he end his public teaching with a list of seven "woes" addressed to the Pharisees, or anyone who acts like them. Among them is this warning of doom, not for committing some actual harm (as stated in the other woes) but for having neglected the weighty matters of the law, justice, and mercy.

The same principles underlie our Lord's teaching on prayer in the Our Father, though there he uses the terms for forgiveness in regard to our own need for God's forgiveness, which becomes possible only if we forgive those who offend us. St. James also states this principle in a short form: God will certainly judge us, and his judgment will be merciless if we are merciless. This implies that if we are merciful, then "mercy triumphs over judgment": "For judgment is without mercy [*aneleos*] to one who has shown no mercy [*eleos*]; yet mercy [*eleos*] triumphs over judgment" (Jas 2:13).

Keeping this principle in mind, we now conclude our study of mercy with two parables that demonstrate this principle of showing mercy in order to receive it.

STUDY

The Good Samaritan

 Stop here and read **Luke 10:25-37** in your own Bible.

A lawyer begins this whole discussion about the greatest commandment in order to "test" Jesus with the question, but Jesus is able to evoke from him the answer: the double commandments, to love God with one's whole heart, soul, strength, and mind, and one's neighbor as oneself. The lawyer then asks a further question about how to define the neighbor, but Jesus evokes the answer from the knowledge the lawyer already possesses through the parable of the man beaten by robbers, neglected by a priest and a Levite, but helped by a Samaritan:

> But he, desiring to justify himself, said to Jesus, "And who is my neighbor?" Jesus replied, "A man was going down from Jerusalem to Jericho, and he fell among robbers, who stripped him and beat him, and departed, leaving him half dead. Now by chance a priest was going down that road; and when he saw him he passed by on the other side. So likewise a Levite, when

he came to the place and saw him, passed by on the other side. But a Samaritan, as he journeyed, came to where he was; and when he saw him, he had compassion [Greek *esplangchnisthe*] and went to him and bound up his wounds, pouring on oil and wine; then he set him on his own beast and brought him to an inn, and took care of him. And the next day he took out two denarii and gave them to the innkeeper, saying, 'Take care of him; and whatever more you spend, I will repay you when I come back.' Which of these three, do you think, proved neighbor to the man who fell among the robbers?" (Lk 10:29-36).

Notice that Jesus describes the Samaritan as one who "was compassionate," using a term that refers to the feelings within his inner organs (Greek *splangchna*) for compassion for the wounded man. Yet, this compassion is much more than a sentiment, since it was expressed by attending to the victim's injuries and by taking him to the inn to be cared for at his own expense. When Jesus then asks the lawyer to pick which man was the neighbor, he defines the Samaritan's action as "the one who did mercy" (Greek *ho poiesas to eleos*). This passage shows that compassion in concrete deeds to the needy offers one important meaning for the mercy everyone ought to show others: He said, "The one who showed mercy on him." And Jesus said to him, "Go and do likewise" (Lk 10:37).

Lazarus and Dives (the Rich Man)

The other side of this requirement — to show mercy in order to obtain it — is that those who have refused to show mercy will not find it. This negative side of the principle is described well in Jesus' parable about the rich man and the poor Lazarus.

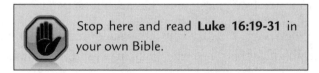

Stop here and read **Luke 16:19-31** in your own Bible.

This parable exemplifies Jesus' teaching on the rewards of the poor and the rich as principles behind a just judgment at the end of one's life. Furthermore, the principle of being merciful or not is a component of God's judgment of one's life, as stated in a positive form in the beatitude "Blessed are the merciful, for they shall obtain mercy" (Mt 5:7), as well as in the positive and negative forms in Christ's judgment of the sheep and the goats (Mt 25:31-46). In the latter scene, Jesus will judge people, including those who did not recognize him, by the standard of taking care of the needy or of neglecting them.

Toward the end of the parable, the rich man still sees Lazarus as a tool to warn his brothers about the dangers of punishment in Hades at the end of their lives. Abraham insists that they have Moses and the prophets — namely, those who gave them the covenant and warned Israel to always be faithful to it. If the rich brothers cannot see the principles of mercy in the Law and the prophets, then they will not respond to living a life of authentic mercy by which they can receive mercy at the end of their lives.

CONCLUSION

We have looked at how the understanding of God's mercy developed in the Old Testament and has come to fulfillment through Jesus. While such a study is valuable to appreciate the depth and breadth of God's mercy, the experience of his mercy is what transforms us.

In the words of Pope Francis,

> God's mercy can make even the driest land become a garden, can restore life to dry bones (cf. Ez 37:1-14).... Let us be renewed by God's mercy, let us be loved by Jesus, let us enable the power of his love to transform our lives too; and let us become agents of this mercy, channels through which God can water the earth, protect all creation and make justice and peace flourish. (Easter *Urbi et Orbi* message, March 31, 2013)

May we all be agents of God's mercy so that his peace and justice will enter our sad and sorrowful world.

DISCUSS

1. What does "fear of the Lord" mean to you now that you have examined it more closely? How would you explain it to someone who thinks it means you are supposed to be afraid of God?

2. What are some of the major insights you have gained through this study of mercy? How might these new ideas change your relationship with the Lord?

3. Whom in your life do you need to extend mercy and forgiveness toward? Remember the words of the Our Father: "Forgive us our trespasses as we forgive those who trespass against us."

PRACTICE

This week, set aside some time to pray the Chaplet of Divine Mercy, remembering Pope Francis' teaching, that it is through our extension of Christ's mercy that we will transform the world.

THE CHAPLET OF DIVINE MERCY

How to Recite the Chaplet

The Chaplet of Divine Mercy is recited using ordinary Rosary beads of five decades. The chaplet is preceded by two opening prayers from the diary of St. Faustina and followed by a closing prayer.

1. MAKE THE SIGN OF THE CROSS

   In the name of the Father, and of the Son, and of the Holy Spirit. Amen.

2. OPTIONAL OPENING PRAYERS

   You expired, Jesus, but the source of life gushed forth for souls, and the ocean of mercy opened up for the whole world. O Fount of Life, unfathomable Divine Mercy, envelop the whole world and empty yourself out upon us.

   (Repeat three times)
   O Blood and Water, which gushed forth from the Heart of Jesus as a fountain of Mercy for us, I trust in you!

3. OUR FATHER

   Our Father, who art in heaven, hallowed be thy name; thy kingdom come, thy will be done on earth as it is in heaven. Give us this day our daily bread, and forgive us our trespasses, as we forgive those who trespass against us; and lead us not into temptation, but deliver us from evil. Amen.

4. Hail Mary

Hail Mary, full of grace, the Lord is with thee; blessed art thou among women, and blessed is the fruit of thy womb, Jesus. Holy Mary, Mother of God, pray for us sinners, now and at the hour of our death. Amen.

5. The Apostles' Creed

I believe in God, the Father almighty, Creator of heaven and earth, and in Jesus Christ, his only Son, our Lord, who was conceived by the Holy Spirit, born of the Virgin Mary, suffered under Pontius Pilate, was crucified, died and was buried; he descended into hell; on the third day he rose again from the dead; he ascended into heaven, and is seated at the right hand of God the Father almighty; from there he will come to judge the living and the dead. I believe in the Holy Spirit, the holy catholic Church, the communion of saints, the forgiveness of sins, the resurrection of the body, and life everlasting. Amen.

6. The Eternal Father

Eternal Father, I offer you the Body and Blood, Soul and Divinity of your Dearly Beloved Son, our Lord, Jesus Christ, in atonement for our sins and those of the whole world.

7. On the Ten Small Beads of Each Decade

For the sake of his sorrowful Passion, have mercy on us and on the whole world.

8. Repeat for the Remaining Decades

Say the "Eternal Father" prayer on the Our Father bead and then ten "For the sake of his sorrowful Passion" prayers on the following Hail Mary beads.

9. CONCLUDE WITH THE "HOLY GOD" PRAYER (REPEAT THREE TIMES)

Holy God, Holy Mighty One, Holy Immortal One, have mercy on us and on the whole world.

10. OPTIONAL CLOSING PRAYER

Eternal God, in whom mercy is endless and the treasury of compassion inexhaustible, look kindly upon us and increase your mercy in us, that in difficult moments we might not despair nor become despondent, but with great confidence submit ourselves to your holy will, which is Love and Mercy itself.

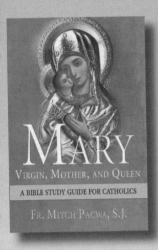
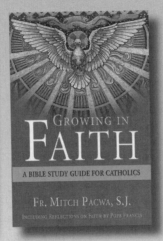
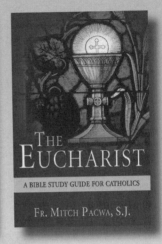